Lela Gilbert is a freelance writer who has authored or co-authored more than 60 published books. She writes primarily in the field of ecumenical Christian non-fiction, and her work includes the award-winning and best-selling 1996 survey of anti-Christian persecution *Their Blood Cries Out*, co-authored with Paul Marshall, and the brief primer on Muslim history and beliefs, *Islam at the Crossroads*. As a writer, she has travelled to Europe, Africa, Asia and the Middle East as well as to many regions in North America. She lives in California and Jerusalem.

BARONESS COX

A new biography by
Lela Gilbert

MONARCH
BOOKS

Oxford, UK & Grand Rapids, Michigan, USA

The author and Baroness Cox wish to express their thanks to Andrew Boyd
for permission to make use of material from his earlier biography of
Baroness Cox entitled *A Voice for the Voiceless* (Lion).

First published in the UK in 2007 by Monarch Books
(a publishing imprint of Lion Hudson plc),
Wilkinson House, Jordan Hill Road, Oxford OX2 8DR.
Tel: +44 (0)1865 302750   Fax: +44 (0)1865 302757
Email: monarch@lionhudson.com
www.lionhudson.com

ISBN: 978-1-85424-816-9 (UK)
ISBN: 978-0-8254-6164-4 USA)

Distributed by:
UK: Marston Book Services Ltd, PO Box 269,
Abingdon, Oxon OX14 4YN;
USA: Kregel Publications, PO Box 2607,
Grand Rapids, Michigan 49501.

The text paper used in this book has been made from wood
independently certified as having come from sustainable forests.

British Library Cataloguing Data
A catalogue record for this book is available from the British library.

Printed and bound in Malta by Gutenberg Press.

Contents

Foreword

It was high time that a definitive account was written about the remarkable achievements of Caroline Cox. Lela Gilbert has gone about her task with great energy, doing justice to her subject. *Baroness Cox: Eyewitness to a Broken World* is well researched and well written. It is the perfect rebuttal of the defeatist view that because the world is a complex and inordinately brutal place no individual can do anything much to change it.

Often, we are intimidated by the scale of poverty, persecution and violence. Headline figures – 2 million dead in southern Sudan and another 400,000 in Darfur; 800 million racked by starvation or poverty, living below any rational definition of human decency; countless numbers caught in debt, bondage, trafficking and slavery – these statistics can so easily intimidate us into inertia by their scale and the seemingly intractable problems they represent.

All too often we feel like the character in one of Robert Louis Stephenson's books, the young boy who plaintively cries, "The world is so big and I am so small, I do not like it at all at all."

Early on, Caroline Cox decided that she didn't much like it, either, but she decided to do something about it.

As Gilbert's account unfolds we see the genesis of an instinctive dislike of bullies, conditioned primarily by personal experiences in higher education – where Caroline Cox battled against Marxist intolerance.

These battles were the ideal preparation for her later travels in Eastern Europe, where the dead hand of Marxism had left a trail of oppression and destitution. During those early visits to Poland, Romania and Russia she began to build the twin pillars of her work: advocacy for the underdog facing persecution and practical active compassion for the suffering victims.

Her experiences as a nurse and as a daughter of a distinguished surgeon would prove to be invaluable. In 1983, her elevation to the peerage on the recommendation of Margaret Thatcher subsequently provided the ideal forum in which to raise her voice for the voiceless.

Caroline often jokes that she was "a nurse by intention and a baroness by astonishment", but for us, her colleagues in the House of Lords, she is without equal in her bravery and dedication. The astonishment would be if there were not a place in Parliament for this rare breed.

In the years that followed her entry into Parliament she needed all her reserves of energy and all her formidable skills – especially during the next phase of her work in the 1990s in war-torn Armenia. In May 1991 she had been asked to lead a delegation of human rights experts from the Andrei Sakharov Memorial Congress in Moscow to assess the situation in Nagorno-Karabakh. Caroline Cox then mounted a systematic campaign to alert the West to the plight of that enclave and to ensure that adequate supplies and help reached its beleaguered people. It is little wonder that Armenia has honoured her bravery and consistency.

Her work in Armenia – of advocacy and relief – would create a template for the future and has taken her to Indonesia, Burma, East Timor, Nigeria, Uganda and, of course, Sudan. Its authenticity has been undergirded throughout by a willingness to expose herself to danger and a willingness to see things at first hand. What better evidence is there than that of an eyewitness?

On my own visits to Southern Sudan and Darfur I have

seen the scale of the attrition orchestrated by Khartoum. With Caroline Cox I have travelled in North Korea. Without such first-hand encounters you can easily become anaesthetized to the scale of suffering and pain. Parliament also listens more attentively if it knows that you are not just reading out someone else's observations.

When I undertook an illegal visit across the border into the Karen state of Burma, the first group of tribal people I met asked me, "How is Lady Cox?" The question didn't surprise me. Caroline is not only respected for her bravery and knowledge, but genuinely loved by many who know that she has kept faith with them and ensured that the world has heard their story.

If you have ever wondered about the motivation behind the carnage in Sudan, or about the reasons why the Burmese military continue to murder their own people, Caroline Cox's first-hand encounters detailed in this book provide many of the answers. It isn't an academic dissertation, a dry-as-dust treatise, but an encounter with real people and real suffering, and it provides a clue to what individuals can do to challenge the things they do not like. The fact that we can't solve *all* the problems of the world is no reason for not trying to solve *any* of them. This story also leads you to understand this woman's extraordinary faith, and how it drives her on.

Albert Einstein famously said that "the world is a dangerous place to live, not because of the people who are evil, but because of the people who don't do anything about it". After reading *Baroness Cox: Eyewitness to a Broken World*, you will surely agree that this is not an accusation that anyone will ever be able to level at Caroline Cox.

David Alton

David Alton – Lord Alton of Liverpool – serves as an Independent Crossbench member of the House of Lords; was for 18 years a Member of the House of Commons; and is Professor of Citizenship at Liverpool John Moores University. www.davidalton.com

Prologue

In the world today there are places that are hidden and unknown; communities that are broken, divided, suffering and silent. Whether it is the result of political oppression, religious intolerance, war, famine, mankind's astonishing inhumanity, or other causes, darkness has invaded the lives of many and joy has fled. These are the people who have no means of making their voices heard – who can help them when no-one even knows they exist?

It is into these situations that Baroness Caroline Cox has brought hope, light and a reason for living. She has never hesitated to visit us in Northern Nigeria – or any other church or country in the world – simply because there was danger or crisis. Indeed, she specialises in seeking out the hidden members of the persecuted church throughout the world; speaking for those who cannot make their voices heard and bringing their plight to the notice of the nations. She has used her position as a member of the House of Lords to the benefit of thousands of suffering Christians in many different countries. Others in the West offer to send aid to those who are persecuted – that aid may or may not arrive – Baroness Cox comes herself. Her eyewitness accounts, her photographs, her moving testimonies and her deep personal compassion speak in ways that go beyond the actual words.

Shortly before a major crisis erupted in Northern Nigeria in 2001 we, in the Christian Church, were feeling vulnerable, alone and isolated. We knew that help was not going to come from the outside world and that trouble was brewing. Moreover, at that time we had relatively little information about the persecuted church in other countries – perhaps Christians in these places were feeling as we did, even though we did not know about them. Then Caroline Cox came. She brought encouragement, hope and the assurance that hundreds of people all around the world were praying. Her first biography opened our eyes to the plight of our brothers and sisters in so many different places. She was indeed a voice for the voiceless and a light in the darkness. Since then she has made several more journeys to us, always bringing laughter and joy. Her journeys continue; she will never give up – she is made of sterner stuff. But wherever she goes the deep, heartfelt gratitude of so many, many people follow her. Words cannot convey the admiration, the love, the thanks and the sheer wonder of the persecuted church: how can one person care so much! Only the Lord can reward this remarkable lady, and surely he will do so.

Rt. Rev. Dr. Benjamin Argak Kwashi
Bishop of the Anglican Diocese of Jos, Nigeria

Preface

When I first met Baroness Cox in England some 20 years ago she was, of course, full of fire and energy, and deeply involved in myriad issues, some of which I have only now learned of in reading this biography. But she had not yet taken up the work for which she has become best known – exposing and documenting religious persecution, and giving direct aid to, and advocating for, the oppressed and suffering. Shortly after I met her she became aware of and travelled to Nagorno-Karabakh, Burma, Sudan and other forgotten places around the globe where people, often Christians, suffer religious oppression, persecution and genocide.

The next occasion when I had a chance to meet her was several years later in Southern Sudan: she was sitting near an – operational and manned – anti-aircraft gun, being interviewed by the BBC over a satellite phone. It was clear that, typically, within a few short years of learning of a crisis, she had, with faith, courage, energy, compassion, eloquence, diligence and skill, become one of the world's foremost authorities and campaigners on it.

Her energy is astounding. One morning in California, while feeling groggy over breakfast after a late-night flight and three hours of jet lag, I learned that, after her much longer late-night flight and *eight* hours of jet lag, she had already spoken at a breakfast meeting elsewhere, not to mention jogged a couple of miles along the beach, and was about to fly out to her next event.

Baroness Cox's faith, courage, compassion and eloquence are well known. But what is often less appreciated is
that her aid and advocacy are backed by diligent research, and
her reports are usually first-hand and supplemented by careful
documentation. As she notes, her work is guided by four As:
"Aid for forgotten people often trapped behind closed borders;
Advocacy for oppressed and persecuted people;
Accountability ... that our message is accurate and sensitive;
and Authenticity, based on personal visits to obtain first-hand
evidence for the purposes of advocacy and the appropriate use
of aid". That is why she can speak not only to villagers but also
to journalists, diplomats and cabinet ministers, and can not
only move an audience in a church or a university but also
pressure reluctant governments and expose oppressive ones.

This wonderful biography gives the story of the astounding range of her work and accomplishments. With others, such
an account, and its attendant suffering, might be overwhelming; but this story is also full of faith, hope, humour and
renewing depictions of the saints Baroness Cox has encountered throughout the world. Few, perhaps none, can match her
personal abilities, but we can learn from her that in our work
we need as much as we can to combine speedy and direct aid
with effective advocacy based on diligent and careful documentation. I hope this book will cause many not only to
admire but, in our own situations, to emulate her.

Paul Marshall

Paul Marshall is Senior Fellow at the Hudson Institute Center
for Religious Freedom. He is the author and editor of two
dozen books on religion and politics, especially religious freedom, including the award-wining, best-selling *Their Blood
Cries Out: The Worldwide Tragedy of Modern Christians Who are
Dying for Their Faith*.

CHAPTER ONE

Appointment with the World

Baroness Cox of Queensbury – Caroline to her friends – is often described as a "voice for the voiceless", as one who works tirelessly on behalf of the world's most defenceless people. But this only begins to reflect the almost unbelievable contrasts in Caroline Cox's life – the juxtaposition of her elite status in the House of Lords and the rough-and-tumble world of her travels. She has, over two and a half decades, made innumerable journeys to dangerous and unforgiving locales on behalf of nearly forgotten peoples. She has seen with her own eyes the worst imaginable human suffering. She has wept, raged and wrestled with her options. The conditions under which she travels are sometimes nearly intolerable; her accommodations far removed from the gilded glory of the Lords' Chamber.

One of the most notorious of her destinations has been Sudan – a nation long torn asunder by civil war, by Islamist violence against moderate Muslims, Christians and animists, and by wholesale slaughter on a scale that can only be described as genocide. One particular episode in Sudan serves as a worthy introduction to Caroline Cox's "Eyewitness to a Broken World".

Because her interests are in the people in the south of the country, before a ceasefire was in place she often travelled into southern Sudanese airspace illegally, flying into areas designated no-fly zones by the Khartoum government. The pilots who flew in and out of Southern Sudan risked their lives to do so, but they left their passengers on the ground with no firm schedule in place for a return flight. If the weather held, if there were no reports of government troops – only then did the pilots come back. And the flights were far from first class. Flying into South Sudan meant shivering for up to three hours in unpressurized, unheated cabins, being continually at risk from anti-aircraft weapons, and keeping a sharp eye out for fighter jets that bore the marking of various Arab nations – nations that had their own unreported reasons for patrolling the Sudanese sky.

It was a risky business, but there was no alternative. The areas of Sudan that needed the closest scrutiny in respect of human rights could not be reached on commercial or relief flights. And the country is too large and the roads too impassable for much travel on the ground. So the unauthorized pilots filed a flight plan with air traffic controllers – but it was a plan that differed from the actual route to be taken. And at the end of the journey, death-defying landings bounced across short and narrow dirt airstrips that were sometimes transformed, in five minutes' time during the rainy season, into treacherous mud slicks.

Khartoum's no-fly zones were located precisely in those areas where the Sudanese government perpetrated its worst human rights atrocities. It was within these zones that religious persecution led to the slaughter of moderate Muslims who did not participate in *jihad*, or holy war, and of Christians who refused to convert to Islam. Here civilian men and boys were killed in cold blood and their surviving women and children captured and forced into slavery; here malnutrition and disease raged; here such sordid atrocities as the mutilation of infants went unanswered. For obvious reasons, the Khartoum regime forbade eyewitnesses from entering these areas, especially those with access to the international media.

Nonetheless, Caroline Cox continued to make the journey. Upon her arrival, she was greeted by throngs of joyful, singing Sudanese men, women and children. Their faces alight with happiness, they quickly unloaded the plane and carried to their villages the supplies she had brought for them.

On one particular journey the heat on arrival in Bahr el-Ghazal was exceptionally intense, even for Sudan. As she stepped out of the plane, a blast of suffocating air pressed against her like a heavy weight. The temperature was well over 100 degrees Fahrenheit; dust and insects were everywhere. Travellers into those remote areas are warned about poisonous snakes, enormous camel spiders, scorpions, giant millipedes and an assortment of other unfriendly creatures.

Baroness Cox is usually accompanied by two or three others when she visits Sudan, and it is their habit for each person to travel with a one-person tent. They sleep in proximity to the burnt-out ruins of a nearby village.

That night, after double-checking the tent floor for disturbing or dangerous intruders, she zipped herself safely inside. She was exhausted, longing for sleep, but the humidity seemed to be increasing with every passing moment. She finally managed to doze, but before long was awakened by a blaze of white light, followed almost immediately by enormous percussive blast. A thunderstorm rolled across the village, trailing behind it a cloudburst of unbelievable force.

The travellers' small tents included groundsheets, a thin waterproof layer of protection from the bare earth beneath. During the storm, rivulets of water began to trickle, then pour, then surge across the area on which the tents were pitched. The rain was so severe that, within a few minutes, Caroline's tent was lifted up on the swirling water gushing beneath. Without unzipping it, or venturing outside, she tried to adjust the floor, pushing against it with her forearm. Eventually the ferocity of the storm subsided, her tent settled back on the ground and she dozed off to sleep. She was awoken by a sharp pain in her arm.

She tried to ignore it, but after five minutes she switched on her torch and saw two pinpricks in a swollen, red arm. She consoled herself with the thought that, as she puts it, "If it was a snake, you would no longer be sitting here, wondering if it were a snake; you would have been dead in five minutes. So, cool it, Cox, and wait until morning – it is only a scorpion, a spider or a millipede". When daylight came, she made her way across the mud to a nearby village where a local doctor confirmed her diagnosis.

The incident – not the only life-threatening experience Caroline Cox has had in the field – left no permanent damage. But it raises an interesting question. Why would a dignified and highly intelligent woman in her middle years, daughter of a surgeon (who is still remembered as the author of an internationally renowned text on surgery), widow of a well-known psychiatrist and writer, nurse, mother of three, published author and appointee to the House of Lords, choose to expose herself to dangerous aircraft and flight patterns, appalling insects and reptiles, arduous weather conditions, questionable food, death threats, and, on occasion, prison sentences for offending brutal regimes?

Voice for the Voiceless

Worlds away from the dangers of Sudan, on the banks of London's River Thames, the towers and spires of the Palace of Westminster rise in gothic splendour, marking the ancient home of the British Houses of Parliament. The palace's picture-postcard façade is crowned by the familiar presence of Big Ben, his great bell forever chiming the passing hours and minutes. Looking older than its years, much of the palace was rebuilt in the 1840s following a disastrous fire. However, some historic areas that survived the fire, such as the venerable Westminster Hall, have been in continuous use since the centre of government moved to Westminster in the eleventh century. Still today, ten centuries later, the two great parliamentary bodies of Great Britain's democracy – the House of Commons and the House of Lords – function inside the Palace of Westminster's walls.

The Lords' Chamber is exceptionally ornate, richly decorated in gold and red. At one end is a throne, awaiting use by the reigning queen or king. For centuries, English monarchs have addressed the House's representatives to His or Her Majesty's Government from this throne, or one like it. Great Britain's history has rolled through the Houses of Parliament as the Thames rolls through England's countryside, in a never-ending flow: through war and peace; hope and despair; famine and plenty; and a monarchy at times beloved and at times berated.

During the twentieth century, the vast British Empire, upon which the sun seemed never to have set, entered its twilight years. After the loss of a generation of young men in World War I and the life-or-death struggle against Hitler's Third Reich during World War II, Britain saw its power diminished, its role in world dominance reduced, and its influence eclipsed. Country after country around the globe, once shining stars in the British galaxy, gained independence.

Meanwhile, the Soviet Union, ally of the West during World War II, emerged as a threat to world freedom during the Cold War years. In the words of Sir Winston Churchill, "From Stettin in the Baltic to Trieste in the Adriatic, an iron curtain has descended across the Continent." The dramatic political shifts that took place during the twentieth century were marked by massive surges of violence and bloodshed. Pogroms behind that infamous Iron Curtain, Nazi genocide, Mao's conquest of China and the subsequent Cultural Revolution, along with violence in Ireland and the Middle East, added millions to the horrific body counts of the World Wars.

Throughout all these upheavals, the dismantling of the British Empire and ever-shifting global allegiances, the British Parliament continued to uphold democracy, human rights, religious freedom and Judeo-Christian values. In recent years, shifts in public opinion and a drive towards egalitarianism have caused changes in the way the peerage – membership in the House of Lords – is established. Today, the women and men who serve in the House of Lords are not entitled to their positions only by heredity; the vast majority are there by appointment. Even as times change, however, and as debate continues about the composition of Parliament, nothing has been lost in the House of Lords' ambience. Authority and prestige still pervade the Lords' Chamber, as in the rest of the Palace of Westminster, along with an unmistakable sense of history.

In mid-January 2004, one of the deputy speakers of the House of Lords, Baroness Cox of Queensbury, stood to address her peers. Dark-haired, sharp-eyed, and with a ready smile, she is woman whose movements, despite her more than 70 years, are marked by youthful vigour. Her style of speech is quick and urgent. She is well known by those who serve alongside her as a champion of human rights, often addressing issues related to persecuted minorities around the world, and particularly Christians who cannot speak for themselves. That winter day she raised questions for Her Majesty's Government regarding recent developments in Sudan, the largest African nation. Sudan has long been a notorious hotbed of violence and suffering, ruled since 1989 by the hard-line National Islamic Front regime which has continued to abuse the rights of Christians, animists and moderate Muslims.

"My Lords," Baroness Cox began, " I am most grateful to all noble Lords contributing to this debate, at a time that is so critical for the people of Sudan."

We can learn much about the troubles in Sudan by allowing an eyewitness – Caroline Cox – to describe the situation there in her own words, as recorded in *Hansard*, the official record of proceedings in the House of Lords.

Tragedy in Sudan

Since the National Islamic Front (NIF) Islamist regime took power by military coup in 1989 and declared military jihad against all who oppose it, the toll of human suffering, with 2 million dead and 5 million displaced, exceeds the combined toll of Rwanda, Somalia and former Yugoslavia. There is now a ray of hope with the peace talks, which need strong encouragement and urgent measures to resolve outstanding problems.

I shall focus primarily on the continuing violence and violations of human rights in Darfur and the unresolved status of the "marginalized areas". I wish first to refer to another concern: the imposition of Shari'a law in the north and Khartoum in particular. If Khartoum remains the capital of Sudan, it must reflect the beliefs, traditions and culture of all Sudanese people. Many are deeply opposed to Shari'a, which violates principles of the Universal Declaration of Human Rights (UDHR) such as equality before the law and freedom to choose and to change religion.

Moreover, the NIF is implementing harsh Shari'a punishments, such as sentencing Intisar Bakri Abdulgader, a 16-year-old Christian girl, to flogging with 100 lashes for adultery, while the man who forced her into this situation remains entirely free from any penalty. This sentence would violate the Convention Against Torture and other Cruel, Inhuman or Degrading Treatment or Punishment, the Convention on the Rights of the Child and the International Covenant on Civil and Political Rights. I turn to the continuing conflict in Darfur, where the situation is so grave that senior UN officials have warned of an impending human catastrophe: Jan Egeland, UN Under-Secretary-General for Humanitarian Affairs, declared that the humanitarian crisis in Darfur is probably the "worst in the world today".

All the evidence demonstrates that the destruction of the primarily African Muslim peoples, through deliberate attacks on civilians by Khartoum-backed Arab militias and deliberate denial of urgently needed humanitarian relief amounts to "ethnic cleansing". That phrase was used explicitly by the UN Resident and Humanitarian

Co-ordinator for Sudan, Mukesh Kapila, in a BBC radio interview on 18 December.

Although he was making the point that the many reports of ethnic cleansing cannot presently be confirmed because of Khartoum's denial of access to humanitarian relief and international observers, other UN officials and Sudan analysts have been explicitly speaking of the "systematic" denial of humanitarian relief, as well as the "systematic" nature of militia attacks on non-combatant civilians with the "organized" destruction of the Fur, Masseleit and the Zaghawa tribal groups.

Also, a Channel 4 news report on 6 January alleged "ethnic cleansing", showing the first images taken inside Darfur, of ghost village after burnt ghost village, destroyed hospitals and mosques and blackened skeletons of burnt civilians. Old men, women and children, without food or possessions, stood stranded in the desert and testified to horrific and systematic attacks across the region. Pictures of Sudanese government Antonov bombers flying overhead proved that those perpetrating the attacks are not merely northern tribes with a vendetta but the NIF government.

The scale of that catastrophe is enormous: MSF estimates that there are about 750,000 displaced people in Darfur; and that in December 30,000 had fled into Chad, with another 3,000 fleeing last week. The NIF claims that "the [Sudanese] Government is firm on fully shouldering its responsibilities of protecting the lives and the property of citizens, and relief workers in Darfur". But all the evidence from NGOs, refugee testimonies and these first media reports belies its claims. Access by international NGOs is severely limited and their activities are very restricted.

And there were reports of yet more aerial bombardment of civilians by the NIF as recently as

Monday of this week. Consideration should be given perhaps to indicting the NIF for crimes against humanity...

Urgent international action is also essential. Khartoum's claim of "national sovereignty" must not be allowed to conceal the desperate plight of hundreds of thousands of innocent civilians or hinder access to them. One can only surmise that the failure of the international community to ensure humanitarian intervention derives from an unwillingness to disturb diplomatic initiatives involved with the peace talks. But that is a dangerous misunderstanding because, unless the international community shows its concern for the people of Darfur, and the peoples of the designated marginalized regions of Nuba Mountains, Abyei Province and Blue Nile, as well as other marginalized peoples, such as the Beia people of eastern Sudan, peace will be very partial and ultimately unsustainable.

All these people have suffered at the hands of the regime in Khartoum – brutality, discrimination and a lack of representation and of a share of the national wealth. At present, they may reasonably conclude that the international vision of peace is focused only on Khartoum and the south. Unless all the people of Sudan have cause to believe that their interests – indeed their physical and cultural survival – are enshrined in any peace agreements, those agreements may not produce a lasting peace. The incentive to resort to armed insurrection could prove irresistible. And, if Khartoum sees that the international community is willing to ignore the massive humanitarian crisis in Darfur and to condone its denial of access to humanitarian aid, it may conclude that it can remain obdurate and achieve outcomes on its terms.

The United States, the other countries in the troika – Norway and the UK – as well as Inter-Governmental Authority on Development (IGAD) countries, must look comprehensively at Sudan's problems if the goal is to secure a just and lasting peace.

Perhaps I may therefore conclude by asking the Minister whether Her Majesty's Government will urge: the NIF regime to open all parts of Sudan, especially the conflict-wracked regions of Darfur, to international humanitarian and human rights organizations; urge all involved in the peace talks to ensure that the wishes of all those living in the marginalized areas are taken fully into account in any decisions concerning their future status; ensure that any funds for reconstruction are conditional on full and transparent implementation of all aspects of the agreement; use their influence to ensure the protection of fundamental human rights, according to the UDHR and other international conventions, for all citizens of Sudan; and, finally, with regard to Darfur, work alongside other EU member states to facilitate the passing of a United Nations Security Council resolution calling for a comprehensive ceasefire, the convening of peace talks that include the presence of high-level international observers, an end to attacks on civilians, immediate and unimpeded humanitarian access, and the positioning of international monitors.

The people of Sudan believe that Britain is uniquely placed to help. They do not forget our historic relationship, which bequeathed many benefits but also a legacy of bitter conflicts, for which we carry an historic responsibility. I look forward to hearing from the Minister how Her Majesty's Government will fulfil that responsibility at this critical juncture, helping Africa's largest nation to move forward from carnage and catastrophe to peace, justice and prosperity. The opportunity for this sea change has not been so propitious for decades; it is an opportunity that must not be lost.

Lady Cox was followed by Lord Clarke of Hampstead, who rose to respond to her comments.

"My Lords, it is indeed a pleasure to follow the noble Baroness, Lady Cox, and to thank her for the opportunity to discuss recent events in Sudan. I pay tribute to her for her untiring efforts on behalf of the people of Sudan and, as the House well knows, in many other parts of the world ... "

"My First Real Credential"

Robert John McNeill Love, a well-regarded surgeon who served in the Royal Army Medical Corps (RAMC) during World War I and as a civilian surgeon during World War II, would have been proud to hear such glowing words about his only daughter. McNeill Love was a great hero in the eyes of many, including Caroline. And he forged a career path that she and her sons would eventually mirror, seamlessly interweaving the practical with the intellectual.

Robert McNeill Love's scholarly grasp of medicine and his skill as a surgeon provided the background necessary for his success as the author of *A Short Practice of Surgery*, which he co-authored with Hamilton Bailey. The book, which first appeared in 1932, was long the standard text for surgeons and is still in print.

It was not this book alone, however, that set McNeill Love apart from other medical professionals of his generation. His tireless work during World War I began in Turkey and moved into Mesopotamia following the bloodbath at Gallipoli. When the British Army appointed him as a goodwill ambassador, he began many a journey that took him from one obscure Arab village to another, tending to the medical needs of the poorest desert-dwellers.

A faded collection of sepia-tone photographs gathered in a family scrapbook reflects the stories McNeill Love later told about his odyssey. He described working all night aboard a Royal Navy hospital ship, performing 40 amputations without anesthetic, using hot tar to cauterize the stumps of limbs, staunching the flow of blood and providing an antiseptic barrier against deadly infections. He spoke of the Arab sheikhs he befriended. He wove tales about his travels among poor villages scattered along the ancient banks of the Tigris River.

Caroline remembers him describing a deadly outbreak of bubonic plague during 1917–18. He was working in a remote desert township when he woke one morning to find himself surrounded by dying rats. In an attempt to stop the spread of the deadly disease he isolated the town – with himself inside – and tried to do what he could to alleviate the suffering. He never believed he would survive. Towards the end of the epidemic he received an urgent call from the local sheikh, asking him to come immediately, as the sheikh's favourite wife had succumbed to the disease.

According to local belief, in order to go to heaven it was necessary to die in one's coffin. The lady was already prostrate and psychologically committed to dying. McNeill Love used all his newly learned Arabic trying to talk her out of the coffin – in vain. In desperation, he looked at his small supply of medicines and found the ideal, if unorthodox, remedy. He gave her a large dose of Epsom Salts. Within ten minutes, she had leapt out of the coffin. And, as he said, she never looked back. The sheikh was so pleased that he offered Caroline's father any gift he would like, and Robert McNeill Love became the owner of a magnificent Arab stallion.

McNeill Love served in the era of the crumbling Ottoman Empire, the death march of 1,500,000 Armenians, the ravages of Gallipoli, and Britain's Mesopotamian campaign in today's Iraq. He had not yet married or established his family. He could never have imagined that all these tumultuous and historic events were setting the stage for his daughter's greatest challenges, both in the House of Lords and far beyond, more than half a century later.

Like her father, Caroline Anne McNeill Love – born in 1937, second child of Robert and his bright and gifted wife, Dorothy – pursued a health-service career, while at the same time publishing academically sound and widely respected books. She says:

> *My first real credential is my father. I've seen his book in many parts of world, in a remote clinic in Sudan and in a Turkish hospital in the Anatolian mountains. I've also found it on bookshelves in Surgeons' Quarters on board ships of the Royal Navy. He served in World War I, in the RAMC, which I gather has more Victoria Crosses than any other corps in the British Army. He spent most of the war in the Middle East, in Gallipoli and Mesopotamia. The fighting finished in that arena before the formal end of war; so he learned Arabic and was sent on many goodwill missions – a kind of medical Lawrence of Arabia. Perhaps my current lifestyle, spending much of my time in remote places, often in war zones, stems from stories heard as a child from my father.*

The Rape of Reason

In the early 1970s, Marxism was casting long shadows across the planet, and long-term fears of a Soviet invasion of Europe or a nuclear holocaust were punctuated by outbreaks of Marxist-based ideological vitriol and violence in universities and colleges. In the United States, the Vietnam War and the peace movement perpetuated well-publicized conflicts, epitomized by the tragic shootings at Kent State University, in May 1970. Similar encounters – not only anti-war, but anti-capitalist and anti-Western – were particularly endemic both in Britain and in Western Europe, especially West Germany.

In 1959, Caroline McNeill Love had married Dr Murray Cox, then a general medical practitioner who later specialized in psychiatry, working in a special hospital for patients who had committed crimes of violence and/or were a danger to themselves or others. He wrote highly acclaimed books that applied Shakespearean insights to psychiatric realities. The

Coxes' first son was born in November 1959. Less than a year later, the new wife and mother was admitted to Edgware General Hospital for six months, having been diagnosed with renal tuberculosis. Caroline Cox's time in hospital became a catalyst for her concerns about the humanizing of nursing, about "treating a person with a disease, not a disease in a person". Some years later, this led to the publication of her widely-read book *Sociology: An Introduction for Nurses, Midwives and Health Visitors*.

After finally receiving a clean bill of health and the birth of her two other children, Caroline Cox completed her Master's degree in Sociology, and was offered a job as lecturer at the North Western Polytechnic, which, after a merger with another college, was renamed the Polytechnic of North London (PNL). In 1971, its faculty of 550 served 7,000 students. After a year, Cox moved up to the position of senior lecturer and was subsequently promoted to head of department. Serving in this capacity she encountered a dangerous faculty and student movement, composed of raging activists, some of whom who had specifically enrolled at PNL to create a Marxist base.

In the years that followed, Caroline Cox endured personal attacks, assaults on her Christian faith, and accusations of fascism and incompetence. The years from 1971 to 1977 were marked by student protests, shouting matches in classrooms, disruption of college ceremonies, and widespread violence. On one occasion, her classroom was burst into by more than a dozen insurgents. Her chair was knocked over and she and her students were subjected to sustained, virulent verbal abuse. Their offence: holding a class on a day when the hardline communist faculty and students, who had taken possession of the building, had decreed that no regularly scheduled classes should take place. There should be no exceptions to the "alternative education" that they had arranged, consisting of lectures on subjects including anti-American policies and "Marxism and the Third World".

Tactics against unco-operative academics such as Cox, including physical and psychological intimidation, lies, labelling, propaganda and character assassination, were repeated exhaustively at the Polytechnic of North London. The department of which she was head consisted of 20 faculty members, 16 of whom belonged to the Communist Party or other groups along the spectrum of Marxist-based ideologies and parties. Members of the faculty who did not compromise or conform to the will of the insurgency faced verbal abuse, physical threats, published libel and public humiliation. Nothing was off-limits to the student movement. The cult-like demands of the Communists even penetrated the seemingly sacred environs of family life, as illustrated by the experience of two of Caroline Cox's friends.

A young woman, previously a student with Cox at another institution, had since married her boyfriend, who was on the academic staff at PNL. Cox recalls a frantic phone call from her former student, asking if they could meet as soon as possible.

Caroline found the young woman in tears, trying to understand why her husband, an active member of the Communist Party and a leader in the student upheaval at PNL, was about to abandon her. He had been advised by his cadre's leadership that either his wife must join the Party, or he would have to divorce her. His wife had refused to join.

The young man's hardened expression and unyielding position spoke volumes to Cox about the Marxists' mindset and the allegiance it demanded. His commitment to the Communist Party had to come first – before feelings, family loyalty or the commitment he had made to his wife. Not only was the academic world a target, so was the traditional family. Aware as she was of the Marxists' malignant intentions, still Caroline Cox was stunned by their hardness of heart.

Robert John McNeill Love died in 1974. During a luncheon following the service of thanksgiving for his life, Caroline Cox was approached by a publisher, asking her to write what was to become a landmark book, *The Rape of Reason*, which described the Marxist domination of the Polytechnic of North London and the ideas that motivated it. The book opened doors for Cox that neither she nor anyone in her family could have asked for or imagined.

In the *Rape of Reason*, Caroline Cox and her co-authors Keith Jacka and John Marks wrote of the Communist faculty and students' efforts: "The strategic aim is to destroy Western liberal democracy by totally discrediting its fundamental values of self-determination, respect for the rights of others, and the rule of law. What kind of society will follow is unclear, except that it will be minutely controlled (totalitarian) and will display a Marxist label."

In fact, the kind of society that would follow became all too clear to Cox in the years ahead. It was also clear to Bernard Levin, an influential columnist who was writing three articles a week in England's most prestigious newspaper *The Times*. On the morning before the book was to be published, Caroline was nervous, realizing she would face serious consequences at the Polytechnic for exposing the situation. She was hurriedly getting her children ready for school when the telephone rang. To her amazement it was Bernard Levin, whom she had never met. He explained that he had just read *The Rape of Reason*, and because he thought it was the most important book for the future of democracy that he had read in ten years, he was going to devote all three of that week's columns to it.

The initial article carried the eye-catching title "In All Its Brutality, The Making Of An Intellectual Concentration Camp". Levin wrote:

> *... I opened [the book] at random and within two minutes I had realized that it was a very serious work. Indeed, I read it through then and there and concluded it was one of the most serious books I had had in my hands for many years and that even more serious than the book itself and the appalling things it describes are its implications for our society as a whole... For four years the three authors*

*and the other members of the academic and administra-
tive staff with the necessary courage (both the moral and
physical kind were required continuously) fought against
the steady corruption of a place of learning into something
little better than an intellectual concentration camp ... I
shall continue the subject tomorrow.*

The second article concluded:

*What exactly has happened at the Polytechnic of North
London? You can find out, in horrible detail, by reading*
Rape of Reason *and I hope many people will. I can sum-
marize it, however, by saying that what has happened is
that a few people have determined to turn it into a place
where two do not necessarily make four, but forty, or four
hundred, or nineteen and a bit, if they say so.*

*Yet Orwell was right: freedom is the freedom to say
that two plus two make four. And that is why I do not
much care if you do yawn when I begin "Send not to ask
for whom the tolls", provided you realize that it may well
be tolling, at the Polytechnic of North London, for thee.*

(*The Times*, 30 September and 1 October 1975)

Bernard Levin's trilogy of articles made the book famous,
enhanced the reputation of the authors, and gave credibility to
their message. And, no doubt, it played a significant part in the
selection of Caroline Cox for appointment to the House of
Lords.

1979 – A Revolutionary Year

In 1977, Caroline Cox came to the conclusion that her efforts
to stand up to the students at the Polytechnic of North London
had continued long enough. Whatever purposes her tenacity
and outspoken resistance had served, she had not succeeded in
changing the ideological brainwashing that characterized so
much of the Sociology Department's activities. She resigned

her position as the Sociology Department's head. Almost immediately, she was offered a job at London University's Chelsea College as Director of the Nursing Education Research Unit. This new role promised to bring together her devotion to nursing as a hands-on, compassionate vocation and her interest in ideas and academic work. It was not only a relief but a welcome new pathway – albeit one that would soon take some unexpected twists and turns.

Because of her role at Chelsea College, Cox was invited in 1979 to travel to Turkey. The trip, sponsored by the prestigious British Council, was to provide a forum for dialogue between nursing colleges from the two countries, enabling them to discuss their common health issues and to develop nursing research. Incidentally, the visit also brought Caroline Cox amazingly close to her father's footsteps, where he had made his own medical journey in Gallipoli and Mesopotamia.

Once she arrived in Istanbul, she found her surroundings fascinating – a skyline pierced with minarets; streets bustling with people in every sort of attire and lined with colourful wares. The city, an ancient crossroads between East and West, proved to be only an introduction to modern Turkey's cultural and political complexities, not to mention the dangerously backward sanitary conditions in some of the more remote areas. Perhaps most significantly, the journey brought Caroline Cox face to face with the historical realities of the 1915–1918 Armenian genocide. This massacre is denied to this day by the Turkish government, but was freely acknowledged by the Turkish nurses with whom Cox worked more than 30 years ago. Decades later, she would refer to this experience in the House of Lords:

> I hope passionately that Turkey will understand the damage being done to many of its own people by its attempts to continue to deny historical truth. Some years ago, I had the pleasure of visiting Turkey to undertake a professional programme of lectures on nursing and health care. I found many of my colleagues were fully aware of the genocide,

*freely admitted it and expressed their wish that their gov-
ernment would do so, so that they could live honestly with
themselves as Turkish citizens and build good relations
based on reconciliation with their Armenian neighbours.
Until and unless the truth is recognized, the many decent,
honest and principled people of Turkey will have to endure
a schizophrenic existence to their own discomfort and at
the cost of international peace and justice.*

1979 marked the broadening of Caroline Cox's world. Even as
she moved steadily towards the international role that was yet
to reveal itself, three world events transpired that would
change her life and transform her world view.

In 1979, in the midst of grim economic forecasts and
endless friction between government, trade unions and indus-
tries, Margaret Thatcher became Great Britain's first female
prime minister. Her mandate was to reduce the socialism that
conservatives thought was paralyzing to the British economy.
Like Cox, Thatcher was deeply critical of Marxism, communism, socialism or any of their various permutations. And like
America's President Ronald Reagan, Thatcher took bold steps
in economic restructuring and privatization, while holding an
uncompromising position in the face of Soviet aggression.

In the meantime, also in 1979, next door to Turkey and
seemingly light years away from Westminster, a religious and
political drama exploded and its reverberations continue to
shake the world even today. After the departure of the Shah of
Iran, and following a national referendum, the highly regarded
Shi'a religious leader, Ayatollah Khomeini, declared Iran an
Islamic republic. Later that same year, in the capital city of
Tehran, Islamic militants seized the US Embassy, taking 66
American diplomats and Foreign Service personnel captive.
With Khomeini's apparent approval, the hostages were held for
444 days. This ordeal not only alienated the US from its former
ally, Iran, but also broadcast angry images of Islamic
fanaticism around the world.

Christmas Day 1979 marked yet another historical

turning point. In an attempt to broaden its influence, protect the puppet Communist government in Kabul and insulate its territory, on 24 and 25 December, the USSR invaded Afghanistan, deploying more than 100,000 troops. The Afghans, who had been Muslim for centuries, fiercely retaliated, uniting their warlike tribes against a common enemy – the atheistic Soviets. The resistance fighters, taking the name Mujahedin, gained the respect and support of the Islamist world by declaring *jihad* or holy war against their invaders. In the hope of overthrowing their arch-enemy the USSR, the United States began to support the Mujahedin financially and militarily. Their mutual goal was accomplished more than ten years later – the Soviet Union was dissolved. Then the Islamic freedom fighters too quickly proved to be a formidable enemy in their own right, not only to the Soviets, but to their Western benefactors.

Steps on a New Pathway

For much of the world in the early 1980s, these events were eclipsed by the mundane realities of day-to-day survival. Even in great cities such as London and Washington DC, the implications of faraway battles seemed negligible. It would be years before Caroline Cox would find herself confronting jihadi warriors, or the victims left behind in their killing fields. Only after 11 September 2001 did the threat of militant Islam become a reality to most of the world.

The election of Margaret Thatcher as prime minister, however, became a turning point for Caroline Cox. Although she had never been political in her thinking (other than disappointing her father by not embracing his conservativism), it was Mrs Thatcher's political concerns – primarily about education – that would place another key stepping stone on the pathway to Cox's most significant work.

During the early 1980s, Cox chaired the Centre of Policy

Studies' (CPS) Education Study Group. This group, a think tank similar to America's Heritage Foundation, held annual meetings that were attended by Prime Minister Margaret Thatcher. After Mrs Thatcher had given a speech at one of these meetings, Cox was surprised and pleased to see her hold up a copy of Jacka, Marks and Cox's *The Rape of Reason*, declaring to the audience, "If you haven't read this book, you should!" She went on to provide a brilliant synopsis of the book's theme.

On a dark and drizzly Friday afternoon in mid-December 1982, Caroline was driving her car through London, barely moving as she passed the Palace of Westminster in heavy traffic. Glancing up at the Houses of Parliament, a random thought went through her mind: *What a pity there aren't more nurses in there.* She had long thought that too much money was being spent on high-end medical technology at the expense of hands-on nursing with its personal touch. Meanwhile, care for the elderly, the dying, the chronically sick and the mentally handicapped was being diminished because of poor funding. It was a simple equation: cutbacks in nursing meant patients would suffer. And nurses' pay was pathetically inadequate. She had expressed her views forcibly and clearly in writing to her MP. Now, as the House of Lords receded in her rear-view mirror, she reflected sadly that she knew of only one nurse who was a peer in that noble institution, and there probably wouldn't be another in the foreseeable future.[1]

That weekend she was preoccupied with putting the finishing touches to her textbook *Sociology for Nurses*. On Monday morning she dropped the manuscript off at Butterworth's and, with a satisfying sense of finality, returned gratefully to her home and family. Now that she had finished her book, she told Murray and the family she was going to "cut out all the extras and just enjoy my job, my family and the simple life".

It was bliss. At Chelsea College the next day she felt completely relaxed. She returned home to an evening of shopping, cooking and family life. As was her habit, she flicked through her telephone message book to see if she was needed to play a squash match for her team. It was then that she caught sight of a new note: "Please ring 10 Downing Street".

Caroline Cox's "simple life" had lasted all of 22 hours.

She was puzzled by the request but grateful that the caller had left the phone number, as it wasn't one she was likely to find in her address book. "I had no idea what it was about," she said later. She dialled the number, to be greeted by a well-modulated female voice. "Thank you for calling back. The Prime Minister wonders if you could possibly spare the time to call in and see her over the next few days."

"Of course," she responded, hoping her voice didn't betray the shock she was feeling. The woman enquired, "How about 4:45 tomorrow afternoon?" After agreeing on the time, Caroline tactfully enquired, "May I ask what this is regarding?" With the formidable presence of Margaret Thatcher looming large in her imagination, she added, "I don't mind coming with an open mind, but I'd rather not come with an *empty* mind!"

The refusal was polite, but emphatic. "I'm sorry; I have no further information for you. We look forward to seeing you at 4:45 tomorrow afternoon."

On 8 December 1982, upon first arriving at the historic home of Britain's prime ministers, Caroline apprehensively touched the doorbell on the black-panelled door, taking note of the brass number "10". Her heart was pounding. Once inside, she paced round a waiting room, occupying herself by examining the paintings. Before long the double doors swung open and a gentleman in formal attire announced, "The Prime Minister will see you now."

Taking a deep breath, she made her way through the portal. Margaret Thatcher thanked her warmly for coming, and said, "Please sit down. I'll come straight to the point, because I believe in coming straight to the point. I've read some of your books on education and I'm preparing a list of names to give to Her Majesty the Queen for recommendations for life peerages. May I put your name on that list?"

Caroline was stunned. She'd had no inkling this could be the purpose of the meeting – not in her grandest dreams. She had no active involvement in politics, and was not, in fact, even a member of the Conservative Party. Nonetheless, Mrs Thatcher made it perfectly clear that, having read some of Caroline Cox's writings about education, she intended to appoint her to the House of Lords. And Thatcher was very fair, saying that she hoped Caroline would support her party on education, but she knew Caroline did not always agree with the Conservatives' health policy. So she reassured her, "You always have the freedom to speak and to vote according to your conscience."

For a woman with no political aspirations or parliamentary ambitions it was a breathtaking moment – unexpected and unsolicited. She had rehearsed no response. Her sense of trepidation was profound, but so was her respect for both the opportunity and the woman who had offered it to her. In the days that followed, she chose the title Baroness Cox of Queensbury, finding herself, as she often describes it now, "a nurse by intention and a baroness by astonishment".

So it was that Caroline Cox entered the august world of Westminster, where she went on to serve, for 20 years, as a deputy speaker in the House of Lords. Her initial appointment was based on her expertise as a nurse and an educator and as an opponent of ideological Communism. But it wasn't long before a new passion tugged at her heart. She calls it being a "voice for the voiceless", and soon it because her *raison d'être*. For her it was more than a feeling; it was a spiritual mandate. "Speak up," an ancient Hebrew proverb exhorts, "for those who cannot speak for themselves, for the rights of all who are destitute. Speak up and judge fairly; defend the rights of the poor and needy."

Solidarity with the Polish People

The Communist-inspired uprisings at the Polytechnic of North London had provided Caroline Cox with an exceptionally close look at the ideological belief system of Marxism and its adherents' attempts to transform the world in their image. She assumed she had seen more than her fair share of Marxism by the time she left PNL and moved on to Chelsea College. In fact, no matter how instructive, it had been only the briefest introduction. Disturbing, degrading and at times brutal as the confrontations at PNL may have been, Caroline Cox was about to see the Communist system at work more closely than she ever had before, and in a far more virulent form.

Mindy Belz has written in *World Magazine*: "Having accurately characterized the problems with Marxism, she set about to help its victims behind the Iron Curtain. She signed on as a patron of the Medical Aid for Poland Fund. The work took her across Europe for weeks at a time, eating and sleeping out of delivery trucks as the relief group brought medicine and other supplies to the dispossessed in Poland, Romania, and Russia."

Five years after leaving the chaotic environment of the Polytechnic of North London, in June 1982 Caroline Cox was making her way across Europe in a rattling 32-tonne supply truck, heading for the infamous border that then separated East from West. After nine hours of exhausting searches by unsmiling border officials, she and the driver eventually passed the heavily guarded checkpoints and navigated the big vehicle through poorly lit, poverty-stricken Polish streets. There Caroline Cox became an eyewitness to a world governed by the ideas that PNL's faculty and students had so aggressively promoted during their "occupation". Their tactics – intimidation, abuse, character assassination, twisted truths and blatant lies – had been applied unmercifully in the Eastern Bloc, enforced by totalitarian leaders against those who refused to submit to their claims or surrender to their authority.

In 1983, Baroness Cox of Queensbury began to meet dissidents, one by one, many of whom were devout Christians who would become prisoners of conscience in Poland, Romania and the Soviet Union. She visited their homes. She listened to their stories. Later she watched from afar, taking note as those dissidents' faith, their devotion to family and their fierce commitment to truth was tested by the force of the fist, the barrel of a gun, or the torturer's cell. She was grieved. She was enraged. She began to speak on their behalf.

POLAND, ROMANIA, RUSSIA

Scale 1: 19,500,000
Lambert Conformal Conic Projection,
standard parallels 40°N and 56°N

300 Kilometers

300 Miles

Boundary representation is
not necessarily authoritative.

CHAPTER TWO

Poland, Romania, Russia – The Iron Hand of Communism

Beneath a pale sky on 8 April 2005, St Peter's Square was a sea of grey, black and cardinal red. The air was filled with the quiet murmur of voices and the flutter of pigeon wings. As if searching for words of hope, a persistent wind moved across the pages of the Holy Gospel, which rested on top of the simple wooden coffin.

In the days surrounding the funeral of Pope John Paul II, Rome's streets and avenues teemed with pilgrims. In fact, according to the British newspaper the *Guardian*, an estimated two million of them had travelled from Poland, determined to pay their final respects to the world's first Polish pope, former Krakow priest Karol Wojtyla.

During his pontificate, John Paul II had spoken words of courage, faith and love to countless lands, in innumerable languages. But he left behind a specific legacy in his beloved homeland. And the Poles remembered. Like most of Eastern Europe, since the end of World War II and the Yalta Treaty, Poland had been clenched within the iron fist of Soviet authority. Personal freedom, truth and justice vanished, food was scarce, and opportunity for change was apparently non-existent. Then came 2 June 1979, when the Polish Pope returned to his homeland, kissed the soil on arrival, and declared a message that reverberated with hope. Papal biographer George Weigel describes the scene:

> *Rebuilt Warsaw was a grim, gray place, its skyline dominated by the Palace of Culture and Sciences, a garish*

communist baroque confection given to the city by Stalin. The city's grayness too often matched the people's mood. Now, for the Pope, Warsaw had come alive, visually and spiritually. Thousands of pilgrims had been welcomed into the homes of strangers. Every church in the city had remained open overnight to give shelter to those who could not find places elsewhere ... the city had been transformed by homemade decorations. The windows and porches of the drab apartment blocks along the roads John Paul would travel had been turned into shrines and altars bedecked with flowers, flags and photographs of the Pope. As the papal motorcade moved slowly along the street, bouquets were thrown in the Pope's path while the crowd broke out in songs, cheers, and, in some cases, uncontrollable tears ...

"You must be strong, dear brothers and sisters," he told his countrymen and women. "You must be strong with the strength of faith ... Today more than in any other age you need this strength.

"You must be strong with the strength of hope, hope that brings the perfect joy of life and doesn't not allow us to grieve the Holy Spirit.

"You must be strong with love, which is stronger than death ...

"So I beg you: never lose your trust, do not be defeated, do not be discouraged ...

"I beg you: have trust, and ... always seek spiritual power from Him from whom countless generations of our fathers and mothers have found it. Never detach yourselves from Him. Never lose your spiritual freedom ... "

Poland: Light in the Darkness

As we have seen, 1979 was a year of beginnings – for better or worse. In 1979, Pope John Paul II made his first visit to Poland following his investiture, and this marked yet another change, although it was a change that was slowly kindled. His visit sparked the fire of *Solidarnosc* – Solidarity, the trade union founded by Lech Walesa. Solidarity's defiant dock strikes, Walesa's imprisonment, the indomitable spirit and support of the Polish people and relentless pressure from the Vatican eventually led to the downfall of the Communist regime's "culture of the lie" in Poland. The decade that followed the Holy Father's visit was marked with violent upheaval and stubborn resistance.

It was during that decade, four years after the Pope's groundbreaking visit to Poland, that Caroline Cox also became involved with Poland's struggle for freedom. As a member of the House of Lords, she was invited to serve as a patron of Medical Aid for Poland, an organization that had been set up in response to an urgent plea from Lech Walesa. Medical Aid for Poland's mission was to procure and deliver such basic medical needs as needles, syringes, bandages, intravenous fluids, catheters, basic medicines, anaesthetics and baby formula. Money was collected, necessary products were either purchased or donated, and the cargo was transported by lorry across Europe into Poland. A few weeks after agreeing to serve as a patron, Caroline Cox suggested that she would like to travel occasionally with the delivery trucks into Poland.

"I asked to do so for two reasons," she recalls with a flash of defiance. "First, to ensure they got through to where they were most needed; and also to be able to say 'I have been, I have seen, and this is how it really is'."

Here were sown the seeds of principles that have undergirded all of Caroline Cox's humanitarian endeavours, which, she explains, "are based on the foundations of four As: *Aid* for forgotten and neglected people often trapped behind closed borders, frequently not served by major aid organizations for security or political reasons; *Advocacy* for oppressed and persecuted people; *Accountability* to those for whom we speak, that our message is accurate and sensitive – and also accountability to supporters that they know what we have done and what they have made possible; and *Authenticity*, based on personal visits to obtain first-hand evidence for purposes of advocacy and the appropriate use of aid".

Over the next eight years, there would be twelve trips to affirm those principles. Some took place in the dead of winter; all of them were journeys into the eerie world of totalitarian control. During those visits, Cox saw the communistic ideas and ideals once so enthusiastically promoted at the Polytechnic of North London now threatening to stifle Poland's spiritual, intellectual and national impulses as well as the very lives of the Polish people. The system was indefensible, and would eventually crumble. And the Poles who stood against it were unforgettably courageous and sacrificial – taking risks as if they had no alternative.

The Man with the Black Satchel

Baroness Cox recalls, "Anyone who visited Poland in those dark, dark days of Communism and martial law will tell you that fear was tangible the moment you crossed the Iron Curtain. There were tanks, there were watchtowers with the guns pointing inward, there were dogs. You felt yourself in a vast prison of free spirits." One senses, as she speaks, that her outrage towards the Marxist system contributed to her desire not only to aid the people of Poland, but to challenge the system that oppressed them.

The secret police system was indeed ubiquitous – tapping phones, stalking, intimidating and at times detaining and arresting those who stepped beyond the boundaries the state would tolerate. On one early trip, Caroline Cox found herself trailed by a man, clearly a secret policeman, who appeared just as she boarded a train for Warsaw, and waited uneasily for it to leave the station. Although she described it light-heartedly to her friends, she was terrified by the experience. In the following excerpts from his book *Baroness Cox, A Voice for the Voiceless*, Andrew Boyd describes the incident involving the man he dubs "Black Satchel":

> *Surrounded by an ever-growing crowd, she suddenly noticed a man on the platform with a black satchel who was staring at her. She told herself not to be so paranoid; it was only a coincidence.*
>
> *Time passed and still the train refused to budge from the platform as more and more passengers piled on. "Black Satchel" was still there, staring, and she thought, "Okay, Caroline Cox, you're not that attractive; maybe it is the secret police. If so, so what? There nothing to be ashamed of or to worry about."*
>
> *Black Satchel ... was a weaselly, cadaverous-looking figure, clad in a leather jacket, and standing too close for comfort ...*
>
> *Suddenly she remembered her growing collection of Solidarity badges – the little red and white metal enamel badges had been showered on her at the various places she had visited. Each bore the crest of a local organization, which would both chart her visit and incriminate those she had met. She swallowed hard and composed herself, trying to maintain her sang-froid for the sake of Black Satchel ...*
>
> *The train had been standing at the platform for almost an hour and still showed no sign of moving, so she thought maybe she should get off and try to find her way back to her friends. But just as she was about to step off, it jolted forward and began to gather momentum ...*
>
> *Taking her leave from Black Satchel she made her way into a compartment with four other passengers, one in each corner. That left two seats on either side in the centre. Caroline took one; Black Satchel quickly took the other. He parked himself down, knee-to-knee, still staring.*
>
> *His secret service credentials were ratified*

immediately by the reaction of the other passengers. They all studiously avoided Caroline's eyes.

She extricated a fat novel from her rucksack and started to read it... After some three hours with Black Satchel staring at her book cover, and she staring equally hard at the pages, at the next station Black Satchel got off. Caroline presumed the train had reached the end of his jurisdiction. She realized Black Satchel would not have invested so much in following her that far, without having someone else to take his place.

She scrutinized the oncoming passengers to try to pinpoint her new minder. It wasn't difficult. He marched straight into the compartment. He was conspicuous by his clothing, which was well beyond the pocket of ordinary Polish people. To double-check, Caroline stepped out of the carriage. Immediately he followed her, placed himself right next to her and started talking to her in English. She thought, Thank you for making it so obvious.

The rest of the journey became a battle of wits. He would fire questions at her to try to trap her into saying something inappropriate, something that would get her into trouble. His opening gambit was to ask for her views on Communism. What he lacked in subtlety, he made up for in persistence. She would evade his questions and try to trap him into divulging who he really was. It was as good a game as any to while away the journey.

When they got off the train, Caroline searched for ways to shake off her unwanted chaperone. Black Satchel had looked unfit and easy to outrun. This one was younger, leaner and an altogether more difficult proposi-tion. Caroline did her fair share of ducking and weaving and back-tracking to try to throw him off the scent. Moving as quickly as she could, she melded with the crowds on the platform until she could no longer see him. Realizing that didn't mean he could no longer see her, she took a number of detours up and down flights of stairs.

She was to be met at the station and was eager to shrug him off before he could catch sight of her contact. Though with that degree of surveillance his employers were probably well aware of where she was staying and with whom. As she was to find out.

The secret police continued to let Caroline Cox and her Polish friends know that they were always around, always conscious of her movements. A woman name Lidia, who was often Cox's host in Poland, never received the letters Caroline sent in advance of her arrival. These letters were meant to inform Lidia of Cox's itinerary and to provide information about her visit. Rather than delivering them in a timely manner, the state placed them all in Lidia's mailbox at the same time – always on the precise day of Lady Cox's appearance. That was just one way the authorities revealed their awareness of everything that was happening – it was a practised policy of menace and intimidation.

Lidia, who had few financial resources, was thrown into a frantic search for food and other necessities, searching in shops that were constantly empty except for bottles of pickled gherkins and vodka. Even after standing for hours in line she was unable to provide the kind of generous hospitality for her guest that she desired. In Cox's view, the hospitality of the Polish people was both inspiring and humbling in that they never revealed to their guests the sacrifices behind the meals they so enthusiastically prepared.

Baroness Cox was also welcomed on frequent occasions by a Catholic priest, Father Alexander Chycki, who frequently expressed his warm appreciation whenever she arrived on one of the Medical Aid lorries. With the help of local seminarians, he assisted in unloading the trucks himself and also lent a hand in the distribution of supplies. Invariably the secret police were close at hand.

Lady Cox describes one typical incident. "I usually slept in the truck, on the narrow top bunk of the cab with the truck driver below, often chain smoking all night long. But on one occasion Father Chycki arranged for me to stay overnight in an apartment. I had just taken my rucksack inside when there was a knock on the door and these two guys came bursting in. 'We've just come to fix a light bulb,' they explained, clearly intending to bug the place. I thought, 'If it's anything it's not subtle!'"

She recounts one conversation with Father Chycki. "He wanted to talk, so we went out and sat in his car, which he parked in the middle of nowhere away from the ubiquitous bugging devices. And what he said to me really gave me new insight into the nature of Communist totalitarianism. He said that one of the things that grieved him most was that it was impossible either to conceptualize or to implement the concept of charity, or *caritas*, in a Communist context because, of course, in the ideology of Communism the state provides everything, so no one is in need.

"It's no accident that in totalitarian societies such as Communism, one of the first things they do is destroy any non-government organization – youth movements, girl scouts – or they take them over. The state provides everything so there's no opportunity to develop private initiatives or *caritas*." Father Chycki said that he found this saddening because as he was trying to teach his congregation about the concept of charity, there was no practical way to exercise it. He explained that this was one of the most deadening effects of Communist regimes because it destroys the soul by destroying the opportunity for the expression of charitable love."

"I Believe in Love"

Despite the state's attempts to extinguish charity, the Polish people persisted in their efforts to help those in need. No one needed help more than the children. And as Lady Cox likes to point out, it is the hope in the hearts of children that seems to light the darkest corners of the world. Andrew Boyd describes a discovery Caroline Cox made in a children's hospital.

> *The courage of the Poles was also apparent in the children's hospital in the historic city of Krakow. What was*

once a dignified building was a run-down structure of bleak staircases and bare concrete floors. At least it was clean, which Caroline noted was no mean achievement, given the chronic lack of soaps and detergents.

On one ward were children with malignant diseases. Many had the kind of leukemia which would be treatable in the UK. The doctors and nurses were well aware that it could be cured, but they had only a fraction of the resources necessary to treat it. So they faced the agonizing decision of choosing which child to treat, and which to leave. Those who were left had little hope. Those who were treated faced an ordeal. The treatment involved intravenous injections at four-hourly intervals. Pediatric-sized needles were a rarity, so nursing staff would have to use large-bore items intended for adults. "It might take hours, literally, to try to get one of those big needles into these little children's veins."

Caroline talked to some parents about the courage of the children she saw in those wards. They told her the story of a 12-year-old boy in the Warsaw uprising. The fighting was at its height, tanks were approaching, they were under constant bombardment and people were dying all around. With his own death imminent, the boy wrote these words on a wall:

> I believe in the sun, even when I cannot see it.
> I believe in love, even when I cannot feel it.

Perhaps it is not surprising, in the light of such vibrant faith, that John Paul II's visit to Poland was empowering. In the spiritual vacuum of Marxism, it was the devoutly Catholic country of Poland that seemed best equipped to face oppression with Christian characteristics such as truth, courage, love and patience. During the most hopeless days, when all seemed lost, Caroline Cox was astonished to see the churches there filled to overflowing with people.

"One morning was bitterly cold, with ice and snow

outside. I think we went to the eight o'clock mass. As we arrived, people were pouring out from the seven o'clock mass. We later learned that the six o'clock mass had been equally full. When we finished the eight o'clock mass, people were queuing and crowding outside to get into the nine o'clock mass. There would be three more masses that day, and they would all be equally full. This was a suburban Catholic church and not one of the big cathedrals – a local Catholic church and a local community. And people weren't there for show. They were really worshipping. We know this because of what it cost them. Just as is it today in so many places around the world, they knew that if they went to church, then they'd be much less likely to get a job, or their kids would be denied entry into a university, or they would face arrest and imprisonment. Yet they exercised real faith, dedication, and, in the service, real worship."

The work Caroline Cox accomplished during her years as patron of Medical Aid for Poland was instructive preparation for innumerable future trips spanning three decades to more countries than she can readily recall. Not only did she work to help provide the donated supplies and cash necessary for the project, but she also used her personal hands-on experience with the beleaguered Polish people as the focal point of her efforts in the House of Lords to provide practical assistance for them.

On 11 December 1989, she voiced a Parliamentary Question, quoted in *Hansard*, regarding "Poland's Medical and Environmental Aid". Here are some excerpts from her statement:

> *My Lords, I am very grateful for this opportunity to raise matters which I believe are of the utmost importance not only for Poland but for the other emerging democracies in Eastern Europe, for Europe as a whole and for the future of freedom and democracy. I am also grateful to the other noble Lords who will be contributing to this debate …*
>
> *Your Lordships may be aware that last week I was travelling to Poland with a 32-tonne truck full of medical*

supplies. As a scene-setter to this debate I should like to invite your Lordships to accompany me in imagination to two of the places I visited. I shall then provide some of the latest statistics which portray the larger picture behind the individual examples of human suffering, statistics which demonstrate the catastrophic proportions of Poland's problems. I will conclude by urging the government to respond much more urgently and more appropriately to the desperate needs of the Polish people.

After describing the needs of one children's hospital in an industrial city, and its specific shortages relating to the treatment of leukemia through intravenous injections, which resulted "not only in suffering but in unnecessary death", she continued:

Now please would you accompany me in imagination to one of the hospitals I visited in Warsaw last week? It is a typical hospital. The corridor in the cardiac unit is full of beds with seriously ill people lying amidst a constant flow of people and trolleys, surrounded by noise, with complete lack of privacy. This is because Warsaw can only provide care in coronary care units for a mere 40 to 50 per cent of patients suffering from heart attacks. Many just therefore risk death being cared for in those noisy corridors...

Coronary heart disease is the biggest health problem in Poland today, accounting for approximately 51 per cent of deaths. It is killing more and more people at younger and younger ages, with the highest mortality in the world for middle-aged men. Many could be effectively treated by surgery, such as coronary bypass. But Poland can only provide for 10 per cent – 10 per cent! – of those who need this life-saving treatment. So very many people, including many who are relatively young and could enjoy many more years of healthy life, will die unnecessarily.

On this occasion, Baroness Cox appealed to the British government for several specific kinds of help. With precision she pointed out that she had had personal meetings with members of the Polish Parliament, including some very senior ministers. Just over a month later, on 16 January 1990, she met Prime Minister Margaret Thatcher to address the same subjects. Two weeks after this meeting, on 1 February, Mrs Thatcher personally responded with a four-page letter, addressing and responding to Lady Cox's requests one by one.

Sharing the Darkness

In Poland, she first came face to face with the cruel effects of oppression on daily life: fear, despair and hunger. And yet she often saw these painful feelings counterbalanced by courage, hope and generosity.

On one trip to Poland, she and her truck driver, Tony, a big cockney man with an even bigger heart, sat down to a meal prepared by their Polish hosts. Unless they were Communist Party members, the Poles had little food. "For all the years I went I hardly ever saw good quality fresh fruit available for ordinary people," Caroline Cox recalls. "It was in the Party's shops, but nowhere else. I remember seeing only one fresh lemon. It was on a Warsaw market stall. We worked out the price at twelve pounds sterling."

One of the church members nurtured a small garden of strawberries. At that dinner, all the strawberries she had grown were distributed among the guests – the British lorry drivers and Lady Cox. "I felt really bad about eating them," she said. "I wanted to refuse but it was their dignity and their pride to give us their best."

Later, as Tony and Caroline drove away, she was reorganizing the lorry's cab. She reached under the seat and noticed a paper bag there. Looking inside, she discovered that it was filled with strawberries. As if they hadn't given enough already, their Polish hosts had hidden away one more expression of their never-ending hospitality. Feeling close to tears, Caroline said to Tony, "How can we even begin to describe what it's like in Poland? How can we make people understand how poor the Polish people are and yet how generously they give?"

Tony was choked up too. In his cockney accent he replied, "All I ever say is, 'They've got nuffink, and they give you everyfink.'"

Andrew Boyd describes her last trip to Poland before the end of the Communist regime.

> *The truck driver had taken a particularly circuitous route and ground to a halt in the middle of a forest in the small hours of the morning. Whether or not they had broken down Caroline couldn't say because the driver was Polish and the limits of conversation were prescribed by their mutual ability to mime. His abilities were limited. He had gone off for purposes of his own and Caroline was left alone. It was pitch dark.*
>
> *Driven by her normal, frantic schedule Caroline often found it difficult to make time to stop and meditate on her faith, although she appreciated moments when she could "be still and know that I am God". Now she was sitting in a cramped, uncomfortable truck in the middle of the night, in the middle of a Polish forest in the middle of nowhere. And she thought, I have no reason whatsoever not to use this time to meditate. Trying to still her anxiety, she committed the time to God and asked him to help her listen to his word and respond. It took a while to calm her thoughts. "Then the words just came into my mind," she said later, "and they have stayed with me to this day. They were: 'Share the darkness.'"*

On 6 November 1990, Caroline Cox returned to a free Poland. She had received an invitation to go to the Parliament building to see the new democracy in action. While she was there, one of the Polish parliamentarians thanked her for all she had done for Poland during their dark days. He then said, "And we thank you for sharing our darkness." Caroline caught her breath, remembering how those same words had come to her during her time alone with God. Not long afterwards, she was awarded the highest honour Poland offers to a foreigner, the Commander Cross of the Order of Merit of the Republic of Poland.

Child of Romania

In her many journeys to Poland, Lady Cox encountered Poland's unique spirituality, burning like a candle that never sputtered out, casting broad light into a shadowy culture of deceit, duplicity and death. Poland was, in a spiritual sense, unique. It shone in dramatic contrast to the darkness that fell over Romania during its years as a Marxist regime. Ruled by the despot Nicolae Ceausescu, Romania set its own course as a brutal police state, even resisting the Soviet Union's policies in a number of ways, promoting instead Ceausescu's own egotistical and nationalistic version of Marxism-Leninism.

In 1967 Ceausescu became supreme leader of Romania. His rule was marked by disastrous economic schemes that led to repressive and corrupt practices, exceptional even in the days of the Iron Curtain. Tight rationing led to near-starvation, which affected much of the population. Meanwhile, an Orwellian birth policy, intended to boost the population, made it the duty of every woman to produce at least five children. As a result, there were more hungry mouths to feed than there was food, and innumerable state-run orphanages, filthy and impoverished, overflowed with unwanted children.

Predictably, within a tightly controlled media, the daily newspaper of the Party, *Scinteia*, reported nothing but praise for Ceausescu. And, thanks to *Securitate*, the dictator's notorious secret-police network that managed to place informers even within immediate families, there was virtually no dissent.

Romania was constricted by Ceausescu's stranglehold for nearly 20 years, but as with many other Marxist regimes of the day, release came at last. In December 1989, a popular uprising, which was quickly joined and supported by the army, led to the arrest and execution of Nicolae Ceausescu and his wife, Elena. Even then, the people who had fought against all odds for their freedom faced a great struggle. Once the borders were opened, and indeed for years afterwards, Romania's poverty shocked the world.

In 1990, Caroline Cox visited Romania for the first time, focusing as she often did on orphanages, hospitals and other health-care facilities. Conditions in state-run institutions had been bad enough in Poland; the state of affairs in Romania was deplorable. Orphaned and abandoned children lived in harsh, cold squalor, evident from the abuse of their bodies and their depression. Scenes of neglect and stories of abandonment were endemic wherever she went.

Yet in one orphanage, a typically inhospitable facility, there was another unexpected spark of hope. There Caroline Cox met a young girl named Dorina who was only twelve years old, bright, friendly and caring about the other children around her. It wasn't long before the Romanian orphan had befriended the English baroness. Lady Cox was surprised to learn that Dorina had taught herself English and could already make herself understood when speaking. She felt an immediate bond with Dorina, and was moved to tears by her circumstances.

"Later, when I came back to Britain," Caroline Cox explains, "I kept in touch with Dorina because I couldn't forget her – she was just so impressive, a very special little girl. And I used to write to her and send her books in English to encourage her English speaking. We did that for quite a few years. Then I heard that she had managed to get a scholarship to study social work.

"I was able to facilitate her coming over to Britain, and I'll never forget meeting Dorina again. I'd always seen her as this rather vulnerable little girl, impressive, gracious, but very poignant in this orphanage in Romania. And here was a very attractive, slight but mature and gracious young lady. I was just so moved to see her.

"What she brought over was particularly poignant to me – a notebook of all the letters I had sent her over those years. Everything I'd sent her was all in this notebook. And then, obviously, she came with very few clothes, really nothing for the very harsh English winter. And so I took her shopping. It was so touching because she said to me part way through our time together when we were shopping, 'This is the first time in my life anyone has *ever* taken me shopping. In the orphanage we just all had standard orphan clothes, so I've never actually been shopping with anyone in my life.'"

Today Dorina Maguran is married and lives with her husband, Tavi, and her son, Nicholas, in Cheltenham, England. She writes of her difficult early life and her transformative friendship with Baroness Cox:

> *I was born on the 16th of November 1978 in a town called Gurahont in the city of Arad – Romania. My parents lived together for a few months after I was born and then separated; they were never married and were living in poverty. They both had alcohol problems. This was not the right environment to bring up a child and they were not responsible parents. My mother abandoned me when I was born and my grandmother looked after me for six years. My mother visited me at my grandmother's but never wanted me to live with her. When I was seven my grandmother was too old to look after me so the Local Authorities sent me to an orphanage in Arad where I stayed for eleven years.*
>
> *The orphanage was a terrible place, it was a very old building, damp, and cold, gloomy and the men and women looking after us were extremely strict.*
>
> *After the Communisr regime ended, many people from different countries used to come to visit Romanian orphanages. One of these people marked my future and helped me to be where I am today. It was 1990 and there were about one hundred children living in the orphanage where I grew up. One summer's afternoon our carers told us that somebody was coming to visit us. We were all very*

happy and waited all afternoon in the main hall to see who the visitors would be. Late in the evening the door opened and Lady Cox together with some other people came in. They were carrying lots of boxes with clothes and food in small boxes and big boxes, and the big room soon was full to the ceiling.

Some of the children jumped into our lovely visitors' arms to get a hug from them. Although it was a normal feeling to wish to be loved in a place like this, I was feeling embarrassed to do this. Some children asked me to translate for them things like: "I want up in your arms" or "How are you, tell me more about you..." Lady Cox saw me and heard me speaking in English; she came to me with her lovely angelic smile to ask some questions. She asked me my name, how old I was and where I had learned to speak English. This memory is still very much alive in my mind and I can clearly remember her saying: "My name is Caroline, please call me Caroline." She used to have short hair then. Her husband had a stick with him and sat down on a box and said, "My name is Murray, nice to meet you." I felt really happy sitting between them and answering their questions about me. More children came around and I remember one of the carers saying with a loud voice: "Don't stay so close to Lady Cox she is a baroness so move." The carer didn't speak English at all so our visitors didn't understand her. It was only then that I found out that Lady Cox is a baroness and I began being nervous talking to her.

Lady Cox asked me if I like reading and she said that she would send me books to improve my English. I was so happy when she gave me her address and asked for mine. She said that she would like to correspond with me. I remember her going to our medical cabinet and writing a list of the medicines needed for the children. Lady Cox gave me a hug and then they left. That evening I went to sleep really happy.

Shortly after this I was really surprised to receive letters and books from her. The first parcel contained easy story books, then harder ones such as Enid Blyton, The Wind in the Willows, and big hard glossy book called The Beauty of Britain. I read them all very studiously in order to improve my English. She also sent me photographs of her family and a picture on which she had written, "This is our house from the country, and we hope you will visit us one day."

I replied to all Lady Cox's letters and told her all about school and life in the orphanage ... (W)e began our correspondence in December 1990 and I have kept all the letters I have received from her. They are very precious to me.

After obtaining my degree in social work I began working for the Child Protection Authority in Romania where I remained for almost three years. I wrote to Lady Cox to ask if there was any possibility for me to come to England, because the British system is very advanced in the social work area. I felt that the experience I would gain in England would be very valuable in my own country. Lady Cox agreed and very kindly made arrangements for me to come to England ...

After the fall of the Ceausescu regime, Baroness Cox was invited to be an observer of the Romanian elections. Of that experience, she recalls, "What was interesting was, again, Romania's atmosphere was very different from Poland's. The Polish elections were very good because the people had come through with their integrity uncompromised. Deeply and passionately committed to democracy, the Poles were able to preserve the fundamentals of democracy.

Romania had been much more compromised. There was corruption throughout – endemic – and the elections, we had to say, were not free and fair. There was a lot of manipulation in the media beforehand and there was a lot of intimidation from the old Communist thugs. Romania's was a totally different atmosphere from Poland's – if you went in blind and you opened your eyes and found yourself in Poland, you'd be breathing different air than if you were blind and opened your eyes in Romania. I think it's probably like this even in the present day.

Russia: Trajectories of Despair

During Caroline Cox's first journeys into restricted countries in the 1980s and 1990s, her response to displaced, deprived and dejected children became a focus of her work, and remains so to this day. Her introductory visit to the former USSR, however, concerned other matters. She went to Moscow in 1988 at the invitation of Valery Senderov, a well-known Russian Orthodox mathematician who had spent many years in the harsh conditions of Stalin's camps in the infamous gulags. He and several other dissidents had planned a press conference to publicize their intolerable circumstances under Soviet rule. Senderov had served many years in the gulag system, and he depicted life under the authority of the USSR's political system as a form of imprisonment. "In the Bible we are exhorted to visit those in prison," he pleaded in a video smuggled out to the West. "We are in this huge prison; please will you come and visit us?"

"Senderov's invitation wasn't one I could say no to," Caroline explained later. But saying yes would involve substantial risks. Technically, holding such a conference could be classified as subversion under the Soviet constitution. Still, she was fairly sure that if they held the press conference and she got out of the country immediately afterwards, it would be safe. Any decision to arrest a British parliamentarian would have to be passed all the way to the top of the Politburo and down again. By the time the Soviet bureaucracy had made up its mind to arrest her she would be out of harm's way.

Caroline went into Russia on a Thomas Cook tour.

Joining her on the long-weekend package holiday was Malcolm Pearson, later Lord Pearson of Rannoch, who had agreed to accompany her. They had met during her Polytechnic years, and he shared her concerns about the Marxists in higher education. But their sense of a common cause ran deeper. "Malcolm has this strong commitment to resist what he perceives as evil," Cox says, "and he always saw Soviet Communism as one of the great evils in the contemporary world." Lord Pearson had been raising money for the dissident networks, and Aleksandr Solzhenitsyn had stayed in Malcolm's Scottish home when he came to Britain to receive the Templeton Award for Religion.

Flying into Moscow, Caroline and Malcolm first caught sight of the tall, drab apartment buildings that loomed for miles and miles around Sheremetyevo airport. Inside their weather-beaten cement walls were warehoused – in poverty and fear – untold thousands of Russian families. To the alert Westerner, those endless blocks of apartments represented the abject desolation that had spread, like a deadly disease, across Russia's 10 million square miles.

Russia was a land whose religious faith and rich culture had for centuries throbbed with liveliness and beauty. Russian music, literature and ballet had long illuminated the world with artistic passion and perfection. Now, behind the vast confines of the Iron Curtain, daily life had been reduced to a grim, monochromatic struggle for survival. Families with several children were crammed into one-room apartments with no privacy and inadequate sanitation. Even the most basic foods were rationed, requiring everyone – young, old, sick or crippled – to stand in interminable food queues.

Throughout Russia, since the Bolshevik Revolution, the simplest joys of life had been sacrificed to the state, and hope had been forfeited to mind-numbing despair. It was the era of *glasnost* and *perestroika*. Many of the Soviet Union's senior dissidents had been freed from the prison camps of the infamous gulag. But KGB pressure was mounting; there was renewed harassment, and fears that the cold grip of totalitarianism was about to clamp down again.

Under Watchful Eyes

Despite *glasnost* – or perhaps because of it – the KGB was still very active. Caroline and Malcolm would need to take elaborate precautions over meeting their contacts. They checked into their hotel, a vast Stalinist edifice, and met their contact and interpreter, Vera, as prearranged. Their rooms were dark and grubby and in all probability bugged, so they kept their conversation to trivialities, or communicated by notes.

On the first morning they broke loose from their tour group and tried to get to a telephone. The air was bitterly cold and the pavements were dangerously icy. Walking was impossible. They hailed a taxi, a large black Volga. That was when they had their first open encounter with the KGB.

An enormous man tried to squeeze into the Volga with Caroline. "He was a typical caricature of a KGB thug: large, raincoat, fur hat." More angry than anxious, Caroline was having none of it. She elbowed him in the stomach and caught him off-balance. Malcolm Pearson added impetus by squeezing in beside Caroline and shoving her along until the intruder was forced out of the door and into the road. As they drove off, their would-be travelling companion scurried into another cab directly behind them, which promptly set off in hot pursuit.

They had been well briefed by insiders, before they went, on the different techniques the KBG would use to follow them. First was the high-profile approach: you were supposed to be aware that an agent was following you and therefore be intimidated by him. The second option was a more subtle surveillance, designed to leave you guessing. Most troublesome was the third option: the discreet spy you would never know about. The man in the fur hat fell squarely into the first category.

Caroline had two items on her agenda: to get to a phone, and to find a worshipping church. They broke this news to the cab driver as gently as possible. Firstly they asked him about the church. Then Malcolm casually said he could do with having a word with his business back in Europe, and would the driver mind taking them to a telephone? The taxi driver became extremely guarded and uneasy. "It was as if every word we were saying could be heard in the car behind," Malcolm said later. The driver fell silent. Malcolm and Caroline exchanged looks and changed the subject. A backward glance through the rear window confirmed that the man in the fur hat was still on their tail.

They had been driving for about ten minutes when the Volga swerved to the right without warning, and the taxi driver said, very loudly, "I've decided not to take you to the church I originally intended; instead I'm going to take you to another church." He veered off down a side street, losing the cab behind them. The cabby waited till it was out of view, then cautiously pointed across the road.

There was a church, and opposite that, a telephone.

Later, back at the hotel, Caroline and Malcolm conspicuously made their arrangements for the press conference. Using the hotel phone, they called several well-known dissidents. *The Times*'s Moscow bureau was put in the picture. It was as if they had made an announcement to the KGB: we know that you know, but break this up and you'll have a diplomatic incident on your hands.

Playing for Keeps

Valery Senderov knew they were coming. Since his release from the gulag, the mathematician had been relegated to working as a night porter in a factory. Cox and Pearson arranged to hold the press conference in his apartment the following day. Among the invited guests were representatives of the independent journal, *Glasnost*, and the *Expres Chronika*, one of the main *samizdat* newspapers.

The theme of the press conference was "Democracy and

the Rule of Law". Twenty people crowded into the small apartment room, which had been stripped of furniture except for a huddle of chairs and a table strewn with copies of the *Expres Chronika*. The delegates knew very well that they were being bugged by the KGB, yet were determined to talk openly about their hopes for a free, democratic Russia. In fact, Senderov's telephone had been cut off by the KGB. Policies were discussed for reform and for transforming agriculture and the economy. Before the meeting ended, the participants had given the KGB plenty to think about.

"It was very subversive," Caroline reflected years later. "The dissidents were playing a high-risk game." All of them knew the risks and were prepared to be sent back to the gulags. But they were worried that younger and lesser-known dissidents were being targeted, and if the high-profile names were silenced, there would be nobody to speak for the next generation of activists. Having a British parliamentarian in their midst ensured a level of publicity that would make the KGB think twice about sending any of them back to the gulag.

Caroline and Malcolm's flight from Moscow was booked for the following day. To celebrate a successful conference, they planned to take Valery Senderov out for a meal. At the first two hotels, the moment the doorman caught sight of Senderov, he slammed the door in his face. At the third restaurant, Caroline insisted on walking in first. As the doorman made way for the wealthy-looking Western woman, she ushered in Valery, with Malcolm following on behind.

As they ate, Senderov talked about his time in the gulags, where he had spent a considerable period in solitary confinement. He was still pale and almost skeletal-looking. He told them it had been so cold in the winter that a veneer of ice had formed on the inside of his cell. When their ration of food was distributed on alternate days, it consisted of cold water and mouldy bread. He used to keep his sanity by working out advanced and complex mathematical equations. Yet Senderov thanked God for the period in the prison camps, because, in his works, "It made me a better Christian."

"Can you explain what you mean?" Caroline urged.

"I mean that through all that suffering, although I hated the system that put me there and kept me there, I praise God that I never, ever, hated my jailers."

Senderov believed that the soil of Russian consciousness was fertile and he spoke optimistically about the future. Spirituality had survived the dark years like a mushroom spore. Senderov explained that when the light was able to shine again, Russia's spirit would respond and grow. Religion had not been stamped out by 70 years of Communism, but was alive, although quiescent, and would flourish again. "He kept this incredible tranquillity and equanimity," recalls Caroline. "His face was almost translucent with spirituality. I have a huge respect and admiration for him."

During that brutally cold visit ubiquitous injustices, both large and small, seemed to chill the atmosphere even more. Certainly the warmth of Russian hospitality and the opportunity to help the dissidents by smuggling their *samizdat* documents into the West made all the risks worthwhile. And just as she had seen abuses on a small scale at the Polytechnic of North London, here Caroline Cox saw the massive abuse of a nation, and its inevitable deprivations, loss of freedom, and absence of hope.

It wasn't long before she learned that – again – it was the children who paid the highest price for living in those unforgiving surroundings. Especially hopeless were the orphans. And most hopeless of all were the orphans who had been declared, by the state, to be "oligophrenic". "Oligophrenic" means, in simple terms, "little-brained" – feeble-minded, or, in common parlance, mentally retarded. However, the director of Kashchenko Psychiatric Hospital in Moscow, Vladimir Kozyrev, offered a different explanation. "In Russia," he explained, "to become orphaned or abandoned is virtually synonymous with becoming an oligophrenic."

Although she had read about the oligophrenic boys and girls and their plight, Baroness Cox had not seen these particular children's circumstances for herself until 1990, when she visited a children's orphanage for oligophrenics in Leningrad (which reverted to its old name of St Petersburg in 1991). She later described them as "well-dressed, bright, lively and eager to talk. Yet they were described to their faces as oligophrenic and totally incapable of ever doing a normal job or living a normal life."

Caroline's first surprise was to find that these "retarded" children were able to compete with her at table tennis. They looked, spoke and moved like ordinary kids. A few were even playing chess. Not only were they doomed to a facility that categorized them as mentally unfit for normal society, but they also faced a future that made no room for them because of their so-called disabilities. There would be no trade school for them, no college, not even routine jobs. The children's categorization prevented them from anything more productive than being cannon fodder for the Soviet factory system, prostitution, alcoholism, or serving in the Red Army, where many of the young boys were trained from pre-adolescence to be ruthless killers.

The next morning Caroline Cox was invited to Leningrad's psychiatric hospital to witness the fate of those who ran away from the orphanages. She entered a nightmare, a hellish environment for the children confined there. The boys and girls were locked in filthy wards with urine-soaked mattresses. Their minds were ravaged by the same drugs that were used to torture Soviet dissidents, drugs such as Sulphazine, which caused cramps and high fever. To this day she has not forgotten a little boy named Igor, with his white pinched face and a shock of dirty brown hair, coming to her in tears and pleading, "Please will you find me a mother? I want to get out of here."

She went out into the courtyard and wept.

Haunted by all she had seen and heard, Caroline Cox

returned to Russia in the autumn of 1991, with a team of child development professionals including clinical and educational psychologists and a paediatrician. Their assessments of 171 children affirmed that around two-thirds of the orphans were average or above average in intelligence. Nonetheless, those boys and girls would bear the stigma of mental incapacity for the rest of their lives.

In *Crisis Magazine* (11 Feb. 2004), Benedict Rogers – a good friend and colleague of Caroline Cox – wrote of that journey's results: "In the dying days of the Soviet Union, she visited state-run orphanages in Leningrad and was horrified. There she found 'bright, able, articulate children' misdiagnosed as 'oligophrenics' or mentally handicapped. She wrote a report, *Trajectories of Despair*, which sent shockwaves through the Russian system. Her damning conclusions could have ensured her a lifetime ban from visiting Russia again, but instead the Russians turned to her for help."

She was invited to the Kremlin by the Russian Federation's Minister of Education, who thanked her for her report and then asked a startling question: "Lady Cox, will you help us change the whole child-care system for the whole of Russia?" This minister wanted to transform the existing system from orphanages to foster-family residences, which had not been known in Russia for the 70 years of Soviet Communism.

Caroline Cox signed the contract with what she described as terror and elation – terror, because she had no money and no professional resources; elation, because here was a breakthrough, an opportunity to make a real difference in many young lives. Then came another request: Moscow's city government proposed, "If we give you the building, will you establish the first foster family here in Moscow to serve as a model for the rest of the nation?" Caroline signed that contract with the same mixed emotions. "Again," she said later, "I had no resources. But what an opportunity!"

By 1994 Baroness Cox, in conjunction with dedicated Russian colleagues, had established the new programme for orphans, called "Our Family", which began caring for orphaned children in family environments. And its eventual goal had already been established – to set up a system of foster care throughout Russia which would provide a transitional residence for boys and girls, many of them declared oligophrenic. These lost boys and girls often went directly from orphanages onto the streets and often found their way too quickly into prostitution, organized crime, drugs and alcohol.

Our Family also began to work on a second objective: to develop proposals for amendments and changes in Russian legislation in favour of foster care. Directed by Maria Ternovskaya, the organization cared for hundreds of children. Since the beginning, Ternovskaya and her colleagues have trained representatives from 46 Russian regions (about 5,000 professionals in total). Twenty-nine regions developed similar projects, and 17 regions approved regional legislation in support of foster care and professional services.

In January 2007 Our Family was launched as an indigenous and independent Russian organization. The famous pianist and second son of Aleksandr Solzhenitsyn, Ignat, gave a performance in Moscow attended by His Royal Highness Prince Michael of Kent, the evening's guest of honour. This event celebrated the coming of age of Our Family and its transition into a fully-fledged Russian charitable organization, independent of Western funding.

Karabakh: Armenia's Battleground

Russia was not the only former Soviet Socialist Republic to be faced with exceptional turmoil. Once the imploding USSR had collapsed, chaos ensued in many of its former satellites. And in the small, ancient country of Armenia – more specifically in Nagorno-Karabakh, a tiny Christian enclave comprised predominately of Armenians and surrounded by Azerbaijan – an unjust and violent scenario began to unfold almost immediately after the demise of the Iron Curtain. By 1990 violence was escalating and would soon once again devastate a long-suffering people, already scarred by centuries of violence, including the Turkish massacres of the late nineteenth century and culminating in the genocide of 1.5 million Armenians in the early twentieth century. Another part of the tragic story was the annexation of Western Armenia, now known as Eastern Turkey. This region includes Mount Ararat, Armenia's national symbol, which still remains captive behind the Turkish border.

Baroness Cox, when invited to a conference organized by the widow of the Russian dissident Andrei Sakharov, first visited Nagorno-Karabakh in 1989. In Sakharov's view, "For Azerbaijan the issue of Karabakh is a matter of ambition. For the Armenians of Karabakh, it is a matter of life and death." Like an enormous Goliath bearing down on a small and pitifully armed David, Azerbaijan began a policy of ethnic cleansing of the Armenians of Nagorno-Karabakh.

Once again, a faithful Christian community faced injustice and grave loss. Once again, the weakest and most vulnerable citizens, the children, paid the most heartbreaking price. And, once again, the need for aid and international advocacy was immediate and desperate. But this was a raging battle, not a cold war. Machine guns ripped human bodies apart, gunships decimated houses, and rockets demolished villages, churches and monasteries. Besides the mounting death toll, an horrific detritus of deforming and disabling injuries followed in the wake of the violence.

For Caroline Cox, as a front-line witness to this war and a lonely voice raised in defence of a just cause, the impact of Nagorno-Karabakh's agony was more profound than she could possibly have imagined. The battle itself, which had begun in a Stalinist context, became transformed into one that included Afghan-trained Mujahedin warriors. The Karabakh conflict was not a religious war. But as Azerbaijan, despite its military superiority, began to lose, it drew on its Islamic contacts to recruit the Islamist Mujahedin as mercenaries. Nothing could more clearly highlight Armenia's vulnerability, lying not only on a geological fault line, but also on geopolitical and spiritual fault lines, where East meets West, and Christianity meets Islam.

NAGORNO-KARABAKH

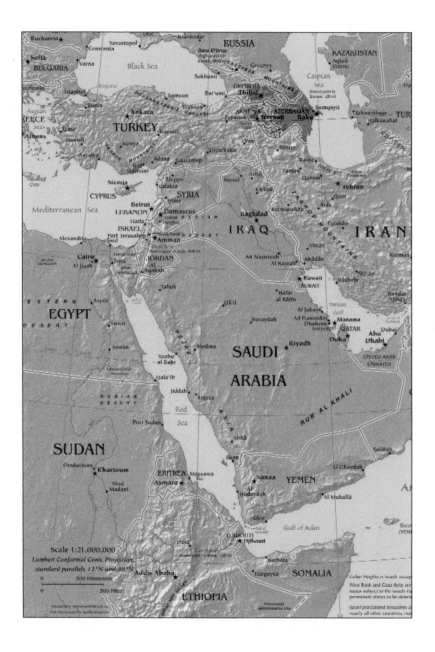

CHAPTER THREE

Nagorno-Karabakh – Flashpoint in an Explosive Region

Behind the church podium she stands poised and alert, neatly dressed in a burgundy suit and white blouse, her brown coif gleaming in the dim light. As she speaks, the scene on the projection screen behind her changes from a jungle in South-east Asia to a group of serious-looking Armenian men positioned near a helicopter, the wind from its rotors tousling their hair. Caroline Cox pauses, and the expression on her face softens. Only those who know her well would notice that her presentation has moved to a locale that is especially dear to her heart; to a story she particularly loves to tell.

"And finally," she smiles, "come with me to the mountains of Nagorno-Karabakh – a small part of ancient Armenia cut off by Stalin in the 1920s and relocated as an enclave in Azerbaijan. Armenia, the first nation in the world to embrace Christianity, in 301 ... "

She continues:

The Armenians have suffered greatly throughout history, being the victims of the first genocide of the last century, when 1.5 million Armenians were slaughtered, and all of Western Armenia annexed, by Turkey. Then, in the 1920s, Stalin cut off part of Eastern Armenia, Nagorno-Karabakh, and located it as a separate region within Azerbaijan. With the dissolution of the Soviet Union in the late 1980s, Azerbaijan began to undertake ethnic cleansing of the 150,000 Armenians living in this little enclave and they tried to defend themselves against impossible odds.

Just 150,000 people – grandparents, farmers, children –
against 7-million-strong Azerbaijan, helped by Turkey and
by several hundred Mujahedin mercenaries.

Caroline Cox shares her memories of a devastating war, one to
which she gave much of her time, her energy, her courage and
her heart. She concludes her presentation as the weary face of
an old man appears on the screen behind her.

Finally, may I introduce a farmer from Karabakh: at the
beginning of the process of attempted ethnic cleansing,
Azerbaijan undertook a series of deportations of entire vil-
lages. They were brutal operations, in which innocent vil-
lagers were rounded up, many were maltreated, some
murdered; homes were ransacked; then the people were
forcibly driven off their land, unable to take anything with
them. During one of these terrible events, at Getashen, a
farmer managed to escape into the mountains. Devastated
by what he had just witnessed, he saw an apricot tree in
blossom and went to it for comfort, as it was so beautiful.
Then, to his horror, he saw hanging from a branch the
body of a five-year old Armenian girl, cut in two. He wept
and vowed revenge. When we met him two years later, he
wept again, telling us that he felt very bad, as he had bro-
ken his vow; for when the Armenians captured an Azeri
village, he could not bring himself to harm a child.

An American colleague stood up, removed his base-
ball cap and said: "Thank you. For the first time in my life,
I understand what the Bible means when it says,
"Vengeance is mine", saith the Lord.' And thank you for
the dignity you have shown."

To this the farmer replied in words I will never forget:
"Dignity," he quietly replied, "is a crown of thorns."

The Cauldron of the Caucasus

Many people in the West have never heard of Nagorno-Karabakh, a mountainous scrap of Transcaucasia tucked inside Azerbaijan. It is a fragment of Armenia, isolated but for a highway that connects it, however tenuously, to its motherland. It is a beautiful, mountainous region rich in pastureland, sparkling with clear rivers and streams. Armenia itself is best recognized for its proximity to Mount Ararat, where the Bible says Noah's Ark came to rest. A crossroads of the world, Armenia has suffered more than her fair share during centuries of war-torn history, none more bloody than the twentieth century.

On the eve of World War I, according to historian C. W. Hostler, Nazim Bey, Turkey's Minister of War, declared, "Our state must be purely Turkish … we must Turkify non-Turkish nationalities by force."

That idea of Turkish "purity" resulted in the genocide that erupted in 1915, when a political group called the Young Turks launched their programme to systematically rid Turkey of all Armenians. It was carried out with a savagery that served as a prototype for the Holocaust. Armenians were burned alive, hanged and even crucified. Women and children were sent on death marches across the desert and suffocated in makeshift gas chambers. When it was over, three-quarters of Turkey's 2 million Armenians had been slaughtered.

During World War I, Armenia became a battleground for conflicts between Turkey and Russia. When revolution at home recalled Russia from the war effort in 1917, Turkish troops began rolling across Armenia and Azerbaijan. Christian Armenians in Baku, the capital of Azerbaijan, battled against the approaching Muslim Azeri-Turks.

In 1920, violence broke out between Armenians and Azeris in the town of Shusha. Of the 45,000 killed, two-thirds were Armenian. Not long afterwards, Azerbaijan, Karabakh and much of Armenia were swallowed up in the emergent USSR.

Resorting to the ancient strategy of divide-and-rule, on 4 July 1921 Joseph Stalin declared that Nagorno-Karabakh belonged not to Armenia but to Azerbaijan, along with the four-mile Lachin corridor, which had been its lifeline to Armenia. The Azeri response was also an ancient one: a population exchange.

In subsequent years, they shifted Armenians to Azerbaijan, where they would be in a minority, and moved Azeri settlers into Karabakh. To enforce cultural assimilation, Karabakh's Armenian churches, newspapers and schools were closed down. Armenians seeking higher education were made to study outside the enclave. To make matters worse, they were not permitted to take up employment in the homeland once they had qualified.

During *glasnost*, in February 1987, the Supreme Soviet of Nagorno-Karabakh called for the transfer of their enclave from Azerbaijan to Armenia. By July they had voted to secede. Demonstrations in favour of unification took place in Karabakh and Armenia, and in a counter-demonstration two Azeris were killed in Stepanakert – the capital of Nagorno-Karabakh.

A wave of anti-Armenian violence broke out in Azerbaijan. Armenians were massacred in the industrial town of Sumgait. Before long, the tide of Armenian refugees fleeing from Azerbaijan rose to what a 1995 Council of Europe Report estimated to be around 350,000. In the USA, Andrei Sakharov warned, "The Armenian people are again facing the threat of genocide."

Then came the earthquake. In December 1988, an enormous seismic upheaval devastated the region, claimed between 25,000 and 50,000 lives and rendered up to half a million homeless. The epicentre of the quake hit a resettlement area for Armenian refugees, and the disaster was celebrated on the streets of Azerbaijan. A traumatized and distraught Armenian population responded in kind. Within 18 months, virtually all the Azeri-Turks in Armenia had been deported, amounting to some 185,000 people.

Deportations also continued in Karabakh and Azerbaijan, until almost all the 400,000 ethnic Armenians had fled or were forced to leave. 330,000 went to Armenia; others escaped to Russia, with only a few remaining in Azerbaijan. There were meetings. There were negotiations. There were vague and unspecified pledges and continuous threats. Ultimately, the USSR rejected the transfer of Karabakh to Armenia and the decision ignited a firestorm.

In 1990 Nagorno-Karabakh – which is sometimes known by its ancient name of Artsakh – had set up its own rival national council and now saw its members rounded up and arrested. Viktor Polianitchku, a KGB officer and second secretary of the Azerbaijani Communist Party, had silenced the press and arrested the Armenian leadership. Within a month, Soviet Interior Ministry troops, backed by Azeri special forces – the OMON black berets – launched an attack against Armenian villages to the north of Karabakh. Villagers were given an ultimatum to leave, so their homes could be turned over to Azeri refugees. Azerbaijan's troops marched into Stepanakert.

Then, in spring 1991, came Operation Ring – a military noose meant to strangle Karabakh and achieve the depopulation of Armenians from their villages and towns. It demanded the systematic deportation of Armenians from the enclave's villages, carried out by the combined 23rd Division of the Soviet Fourth Army and forces of the Azerbaijani Ministry of the Interior, the OMON.

When the Azeri troops moved in, Galia Saoukhanin, a 29-year-old mother from the village of Nakhichevanik, was forced to flee with her two small children. "They killed the population here: all who couldn't escape; the elderly people who couldn't run. My brother was killed. My brother-in-law was killed. It changed my destiny and my soul. For months my children were crying without stopping. I have a terrible fear inside me. I dream every night how I am going to escape and where I am going to keep my children."

No one could have been prepared for the savagery of the Azeri onslaught. Medical worker Movses Poghossian followed behind the conflict, picking up the human remains of atrocity after atrocity. "There are bodies without eyes, without ears... they are cutting crosses, they cut off hands."

It was against this backdrop of violence that Baroness Cox was introduced to the tragedy of Nagorno-Karabakh. She later described her first encounter, in May 1991.

I had been asked to lead a delegation of human rights experts from the Andrei Sakharov Memorial Congress in Moscow to obtain evidence of the violations of human rights inflicted on the Armenians of Artsakh during Azerbaijan's brutal policy of "Operation Ring".

Having heard the evidence of the suffering of the Armenians deported from places such as Getashen, Martunashen and Berdadzor, I and my colleagues decided that we needed to hear the Azeri version of events. However, the Azeris refused us permission to fly to Stepanakert, so we agreed amongst ourselves to do the next best thing: to walk across the border with a white flag.

We flew by helicopter to Voskepar, where we left the friendly pilots to undertake the crazy mission of walking into Azerbaijan, where we were met by very hostile OMON and regular army commandeers who were not very pleased by our unorthodox approach.

However, it was essential to hear both the Armenian and Azeri points of view. As human rights activists, we try to follow the example of Andrei Sakharov who always worked on the side of the victim. We therefore had to find the evidence to show who are the primary aggressors and who are the victims of aggression. Our visit to Voskepar provided this evidence and made it possible for us to begin our advocacy on behalf of the Armenian people and especially of those suffering in the war for Artsakh.

When we returned to Britain, we were able to give

an interview with the BBC, who said they would not have broadcast our report if we had not heard the Azeri as well as the Armenian views.

Running Drugs in a War Zone

After her dramatic introduction to Nagorno-Karabakh, Caroline Cox was to return again and again during the war. As the fighting ground on, one of the most troubling elements for her was the lack of medical supplies for the wounded. During a visit to Stepanakert's hard-hit hospital in January 1991, she confirmed for herself horror stories she'd heard of surgical operations without anaesthetics, deadly infections without antibiotics, primitive conditions without electricity or running water. She witnessed the pitiful conditions endured by the patients. As she was a nurse, these matters were particularly disturbing for her, since she was fully aware of what could and should have been available to Armenian medics.

Karabakh's military authorities gave Caroline Cox a list before she left the country of their most urgent priorities, including hard drugs such as morphine, and cocaine powder for eye injuries. Once she was back in England, she made calls to anyone and everyone who might help with funding, procurement and transport. Before long she became, in her own words, "an international drugs carrier".

The Home Office gave her a licence to purchase and export the restricted drugs. In January 1992, the medications were packed into two substantial plywood crates, marked "Fragile, Handle with Care", and Caroline Cox was faced with the challenge of transporting them to Armenia. After a rather unorthodox journey, Cox, her travelling companions and the medications arrived in Yerevan on a cold, crisp day, where they were transferred to a military helicopter that would take them to Stepanakert. Joining them was a medical team and a worried-looking Zori Balayan, the elected representative for Karabakh on the Supreme Soviet of the Soviet Union, as well as a physician and the distinguished author of more than 50 books. He reported that the Azeris had escalated the conflict significantly in recent days with the use of Grad (BM21) missiles.

Grads had been used to devastating effect in Afghanistan and were banned by international convention. They were fired in multiples of 40. If they exploded outside a building they did major damage to the exterior. If they penetrated the building's wall, the entire structure was shattered from within by a whirlwind of shrapnel. In Shaumyan, to the north of Karabakh, two schools had been pulverized. Because of the devastating injuries the Grads had caused, the Cox party made a stop in Shaumyan to offload some morphine and other painkilling drugs.

As the helicopter took off again on its way to Stepanakert, the cloud cover was so thick and visibility so poor that the pilot soon announced they could not continue; they would have to sit out the bad weather on the ground. He located a break in the clouds and landed at Horator. There Caroline and her colleagues found themselves stranded in Azeri-held territory. The only way out was to walk. She and the others were all too aware of the dangers of exposure – both to the frigid weather and to snipers. After many hours' walking through the forest and thick snow, they found their way to a local village, which, providentially, was Armenian. The villagers invited them into their homes to eat, drink and thaw out around log fires. A stone was later set up to commemorate the walk, which the locals called "Cox Way".

The following day, the group completed its journey to Stepanakert. Just twelve days had passed since Caroline Cox's last visit to the hospital. She was saddened to find that conditions were even worse than before because the facility had come under heavy fire. Alazan rockets and artillery shells had struck even as surgeons were performing an operation. The separate maternity hospital had also taken a direct hit. Mothers and babies had been transferred to the basement, where they were still being cared for in freezing, damp conditions that invited hypothermia. A number of mothers had given birth prematurely. The drugs and medical supplies were immediately distributed by the hospital's grateful staff. From that day on, no further deaths were reported from pain-induced shock during surgery without anaesthetic.

It would be four more months before the Red Cross was able to follow in Baroness Cox's footsteps and enter Karabakh. She later described the mission:

> *During 1991, I visited Azerbaijan in July, to obtain a fuller version of Azerbaijan's policies; I then travelled to Armenia and Karabakh in October. In December, full-scale war broke out. I was appalled by the situation. There was constant bombardment of Stepanakert from Shushi. Electricity had been cut off by Azerbaijan, so women and children were trapped in basements and cellars, with no light, heat or running water.*
>
> *In the hospital, casualties of war were suffering horrific injuries. But with Artsakh besieged, blockaded and bombarded, the Armenian doctors had virtually no medicines, including no painkillers or anaesthetics. I could not sleep when I returned to Britain, thinking of that unrelieved pain, so we managed to obtain a large consignment of medicines and returned 12 days later.*

In May 1992, Armenia and Azerbaijan inked their signatures on a peace agreement in Tehran. The following day, an Azeri offensive began. All attempts to mediate in the conflict had failed. Armenia's plea to the UN to send in peacekeepers fell on deaf ears. *The New York Times* warned: "Without political intervention, the deadly little war will degenerate to the levels of Bosnia."

In fact, it already had.

The Battle for Shushi

Grad missiles were launched from the heights of Shushi, bombarding the civilian population in Stepanakert below. It was imperative to stop the missiles. But there was another compelling reason for Karabakh to reclaim Shushi – the town straddled the main road connecting Nagorno-Karabakh to Armenia. Shushi's fall would enable food and arms to go through unchecked. It might even turn the tide of the war.

The battle for Shushi was, however, a military strategist's nightmare, for two reasons. The assault on the fortress town would put at risk a significant portion of Karabakh's already depleted forces. And, as a treasured historic centre of Armenian culture, Shushi had to remain as undamaged by further conflict as possible.

Karabakh's strategists devised a ruse – they persuaded the Azeris that they were being attacked by an enormous force by driving their few vehicles round and round, revving their engines and making as much noise and clamour as they could muster. A corridor was left open for Azeri soldiers and remaining civilians to escape. As hoped, they fled en masse, resulting in fewer casualties on both sides than had been feared. The official figure for Armenian losses was 32 dead and 36 wounded.

The fall of Shushi was a military triumph. From Caroline Cox's perspective, the whole conflict had acquired a biblical dimension. "It was like Gideon driving out the Midianites: the odds were impossible," she smiles joyfully as she relates the story. "The whole of Karabakh had a remaining population of some 140,000, including women and children. They were fighting against more than 7 million Azeris, assisted by battle-hardened mercenaries. And yet they prevailed."

The following month an election in Azerbaijan did not bode well for the Armenians. It swept to power the extremist Azerbaijani Popular Front, with a mandate to settle the Karabakh problem. A renewed military offensive was launched, with the advice and assistance of 40 senior Turkish army officers who had all taken "early retirement" from their responsibilities to Ankara. According to Karabakh, Turkish participation in the conflict ran deeper. Turkey was sustaining a crippling blockade of Armenia, and it was claimed that captured weapons bore the Turkish insignia. Some 40 planeloads of Turkish weapons per day were said to be bound for Baku; the bodies of six soldiers had been identified as Turks, and a tank had been knocked out bearing the Turkish "Grey Wolves" insignia.

But there were even more disturbing reports about Muslim forces. Azerbaijan had recruited up to 3,000 mercenaries, including Mujahedin veterans of the Afghan conflict, jihadists who were eager for fresh opportunities to drive back the infidel. And if the prospect of a jihad was insufficiently enticing, there was also the promise of large amounts of money – enough money to create a long line of volunteers outside the Iranian consulate in Pakistan. And, according to State Defence Minister Vazguen Sarkissian, in a 1994 interview with author Andrew Boyd, Saudi Arabian funds had reportedly been invested in the recruitment drive.

The reality of a Muslim vs Christian dimension to the war was understandably played down within Karabakh. "It is not a religious war," said Bishop Martirosian on more than one occasion. "But there is a danger with the Azeris using Mujahedin that they may internationalize the conflict and make it a religious war." As if to ward off any further trouble, an Armenian team of restorers was dispatched into Shushi to repair whatever damage the war had inflicted on the local mosque.

In April 1992, Azerbaijani troops attacked the town of Maraghar, leaving behind evidence of unspeakable cruelty. More than 100 women and children had been kidnapped, most of the town was looted then burned to the ground, and 45 villagers had been beheaded – their heads sawn off and their bodies burned. Caroline Cox visited the remains of the town and interviewed survivors, recognizing that the massacre was but one of many such brutal attacks by the Azeris . A traumatized mother told her:

> They attacked the village and started cutting the villagers to pieces. I myself heard the screams of a man who was having his head cut off by a saw. Then we took our children and ran away. The next day we returned to the village. People were cut into pieces, their eyes were gouged out, their ears were cut off. We then saw the [body of the] man whom I had previously seen being decapitated. The saw was lying next to him and all the blood had flowed out of the body. Another man – our uncle – was tied to the back of a tank and was dragged 500 metres. After that we fled to Shaumyan. Ten days later, the Azeri-Turks did the same things. After that I took the children and fled. We walked for 40 miles. We arrived thirsty and hungry and with our clothes in tatters. We couldn't take anything with us. I've seen these atrocities with my own eyes.

After leaving the village of Maraghar, Caroline Cox visited the hospital in the regional capital town of Mardakert. There she met the head nurse who had just fled from the village. Fourteen of her relatives had been slaughtered, and she had seen her own son's head sawn off. As Caroline embraced her they wept together. After the traumatized nurse had finished sobbing, Caroline said to her, "Would you find it comforting to give a message to the world? To tell them what has happened to your people?"

Caroline watched in wonder as the woman's countenance changed, her expression transformed from grief to dignity. She replied, "Like you, I'm a nurse and I have worked in this hospital for a long time. I have seen how the medicines you brought saved many lives and eased so much pain. I therefore just want to say thank you. Thank you to all those people who have not forgotten us in these terrible days."

The days were, indeed, terrible. Forty per cent of Karabakh was overrun and Azeri troops were within ten miles of Stepanakert. Longer-range missiles were being used, launched from beyond the reach of Karabakh defence forces. The civilian casualty rate soared. The enclave was rapidly becoming depopulated. Almost all the Azeri-Turk civilians had left or been driven from their homes. Now, Nagorno-Karabakh's remaining able-bodied citizens were making the hazardous journey to a safe haven in Armenia.

In August 1992, the Azeris pressed aircraft into the conflict. SU25s started dropping 500-kilogramme bombs on Stepanakert and the surrounding villages. By October, their payload had changed to cluster bombs, which are banned for use against civilians under international convention. Also banned was the use of flechettes, dart-like bullets with fins designed to maximize damage to human tissue. Surgeons were soon struggling to remove flechettes from soldiers coming in from the battlefield. But the cluster bombs were far less discriminating. The attractive-looking silver balls, primed to explode when touched, attracted children like magnets.

Twelve-year-old Pailak Haratunian was playing in the woods with his friends when he picked up one of the silver balls and decided to carry it home. He fell. The explosion tore out one eye, damaged the other, injured his leg and chest, and perforated his colon. Maria Bedelian, also twelve, found a ball in her garden in a village near Stepanakert. As she was taking it to show her mother, she tripped. Seven people were wounded in the explosion. Maria's left leg was splintered like a twig and she suffered multiple injuries. The surgeons didn't know where to start. A weary doctor in Stepanakert shook his head in disbelief. "This is not the front line," he protested. "These are *children*."

When Caroline Cox heard reports of these injuries, she visited the children in the hospital. Sickened by what she saw and heard, she gathered her evidence. The more she learned, the more determined she was that the British government should condemn the Azeri atrocities.

Ashamed to be British

Armed with photos and interviews, the Baroness arranged a meeting at the Foreign Office with a senior politician. She pointed out that Azerbaijan was a signatory to the major conventions on human rights and a member of the Conference on Security and Co-operation in Europe (CSCE). "Therefore, would the British government prevail upon Azerbaijan," she queried, "to stop dropping cluster bombs on children, which is a gross violation of human rights?"

The senior politician, who must remain unnamed, coolly replied, "No country has an interest in other countries, only interests. And we have oil interests in Azerbaijan." And he showed her to the door.

"I went back home and wept," she said later, describing her sense of powerlessness and dismay when a government, which might have done something to save the lives of innocent civilians, put oil interests first.

In the days that followed she visited British Petroleum, requesting guarantees that oil profits would not be invested in weapons; that a share of the profits would be distributed among the victims of war, both Armenian and Azeri, and for BP to exert its influence to prevent Azerbaijan from imposing a military solution. British Petroleum declined all her requests.

And as for Britain's Foreign Office policy? As far as Baroness Cox was concerned, there was no way that was going to remain behind closed doors.

She rose to her feet in the House of Lords and looked across the elegantly appointed chamber. It was a setting that would appeal to the pride of any British patriot. But on that occasion, she felt no surge of satisfaction. Before all the assembled peers, she reported her conversation with the Foreign Office official. She concluded:

> For the first time in my life, I am ashamed to be British. I can understand strategic interests. I can understand commercial interests, but I didn't think it was the long-term

interest of any country to let those obliterate concern for
human rights. Moreover, I didn't think the majority of
British people would actually want oil at the price of clus-
ter bombs on children.

A Shift in World Opinion

The Nagorno-Karabakh war began with massacres of
Armenians and what appeared to be a strong Azeri advantage.
The tiny enclave of Nagorno-Karabakh was assaulted by massive military offensives. The Armenians living there decided to
resist, despite apparently impossible odds, and with only hunt-
ing rifles to defy attacks on their villages by Azeri troops that
were well armed with tanks, sophisticated weapons and helicopter gunships.

Indeed, Azerbaijan's early successes appeared to be omi-
nously foreshadowing a humiliating defeat for Karabakh. But
the enclave's fighters, supported by Armenian troops and
arms, fought courageously and tenaciously. As 1992 waned,
the tide of war began to turn in favour of Nagorno-Karabakh.
The military stalemate was broken as Karabakh's troops
moved west and south to bridge the gap between their enclave
and Armenia proper, seizing territory to the east, between
Karabakh and Iran. This would secure a buffer zone from
Azeri missiles and artillery. It would also displace thousands of
civilians.

Among those displaced was a family from the village of
Mataghis, in the region of Mardakert. The mother of the family was the local schoolteacher and her eleven-year-old son,
Gehgam, did not want to leave his home. The boy literally
clung on to the doorpost so fiercely that his parents had to
drag him away as Azeri tanks appeared on the horizon. The
family fled, along with thousands of others, to the already
bombed and devastated capital city of Stepanakert. Gehgam,
in his anguish, wrote a poem about his beloved homeland.

I climbed barefoot the mountains,
To pay my last visit with yearning.
The mountain looked at me and became dark,
"What are you doing, black-eyed child?" he asked.
I kneeled down at the Tharthar riverbank
To pay my last visit,
Tharthar became wavy suddenly,
"What are you doing, black-eyed child?"
I went to our beautiful bushland,
For the last time to pick up some flowers.
"Shame on you" the bushes told me again,
And when I looked at the beautiful sun,
With tears in my eyes,
"How, how can I leave all this?" I wept.
"How can I leave Artsakh?
You as a mother love me and embrace me."
And I lay down on the ground,
Hugged the old land,
And I shouted loud, so the earth would hear me,
"No, no, in our life we will never leave Artsakh,
We will never search for a haven in other lands,
Let Artsakh be our grave.
Forgive me my dear motherland,
That I for a minute thought to leave and get away.
I won't be an adopted child to another mother,
No matter how good she is,
She is still only a stepmother.
My love, my dear Artsakh,
Be a holy parent to your children,
I won't be tempted by another life,
Any heavenly life is not going to enslave me,
I have been born in these mountains,
I will become soil in Mataghis (his village).
I will be soil, I will be a rock,
Only if my village is always alive,
I will mix with the soil of my land,
And silently listen to the voice of Tharthar.

The following year, when the Armenians managed to stem the tide of defeat and regain some of their land, Caroline Cox was able to accompany Gehgam and his family as they returned to their village. His mother silently surveyed all that remained of their home. It had been looted and burned, and all that was left was a blackened ruin. Her face fell, but she regained her composure as quickly as she could. "A house is only a building," she finally said. "And we will soon make our home again."

In June 2006, Lady Cox spoke at a fund-raising dinner for the Armenian community in Toronto, hoping to raise funds for a new school in Mataghis. By September, she was back in the village cutting the red ribbon for a beautiful new school building. She was gratified to see that the boy poet, Gegham, now a handsome young man in his twenties, was there; he had returned to his village to teach in the new school. At the ceremony marking the school's opening, Caroline's eyes filled with tears as he stood before the community and recited the poem he had written as a child.

Turmoil in Baku

By April 1994, almost all of Karabakh was in Armenian hands, consolidating control of territory bordering Karabakh and Armenia. In November, with its war aims secure, Karabakh offered to pull back from the ground it had occupied in return for independence from Azerbaijan. That independence was denied. But on 12 May 1994, Russia and the Organization for Security and Co-operation in Europe (OSCE, formerly the CSCE) mediated a ceasefire.

According to Reuters, 35,000 people died. The war displaced more than 1.5 million on both sides. Armenians began to settle in the territories they now occupied. Meanwhile, Azerbaijan was reluctant to settle its own displaced population for fear of compromising its claim to Armenian-held territories.

Caroline Cox has publicly questioned why there is such a stark contrast between the ways in which the Armenians and the Azeris take care of the roughly comparable numbers of people who have been displaced. The Armenians, afflicted by an earthquake, an economic blockade imposed by Turkey and Azerbaijan and the suffering brought about by the war in Karabakh, and with a population of only 3 million, have managed to find accommodation for all their refugees. Azerbaijan, by contrast, with a population of 7 million, no earthquake, no economic blockade, with massive oil revenues, and money provided by the UN High Commission for Refugees (UNHCR), has elected still to keep many of its displaced in conditions of acute deprivation in camps.

Legacy of War

Caroline Cox's visits to Karabakh continued even after the fighting stopped in 1994. Despite the ceasefire, a lasting memory of the war remained in the form of the many disabled people and the victims of landmines. The authorities asked Baroness Cox to become involved in post-war reconstruction of the most fundamental kind – a clinic to provide rehabilitation. In a recent interview she described the founding and flourishing of that clinic:

> *In the post-war years, we sought advice on the priority for humanitarian assistance and we were asked to help to establish a Rehabilitation Centre. This was especially significant, as the former USSR had no concept of rehabilitation: people who became disabled or maimed by war injuries were consigned to institutions where they were "warehoused" with little or nothing in the way of rehabilitation. For example, life expectancy, even for a previously fit young adult who became paralyzed from the waist downwards due to a spinal cord injury, would be typically about two years: death would result from pressure sores which would become gangrenous and/or from respiratory or urinary tract infections.*
>
> *The Armenians of Karabakh wanted better*

provision for the survivors of this bitter war, both for sol-
diers and for civilians who had sustained injuries, as well
as for others suffering various forms of disability, such as
children with cerebral palsy or older people who had had
strokes.

The range of therapies now provided by the rehabil-
itation centre include basic provisions for prevention or
treatment of pressure sores, with a specialist nurse who is
an expert in tissue repair; physiotherapy and speech ther-
apy; occupational therapies including high-quality teach-
ing in art, music, pottery and wood-carving; sports
therapy, including table tennis for hemiplegics; and a
Computer Centre providing training in IT for patients,
allowing them to become proficient in computing skills
and to surf the web, opening horizons far beyond the con-
fines of Karabakh.

The most recent developments include a modern-
ized kitchen, where patients can receive help with culinary
skills (a valuable aspect of rehabilitation) and a new cen-
tral heating system. The most spectacular innovation is a
state-of-the-art hydrotherapy pool, which will be a useful
resource for treating a wide range of patients with mobil-
ity problems and various degrees of spasticity. It has been
agreed that the pool will be named after David Ahmanson,
in appreciation of the support provided by his generous
family.

In 2005 clinic director Vardan Tadevosyan organized a conference that was attended by representatives from the entire
region, including Georgia, Abkhazia, Ossetia, Chechnya and
even Azerbaijan. They came to learn about rehabilitation and
to take back the enhanced range of innovative therapies to
their own countries. Today the small city of Stepanakert,
which only a short while ago was pulverized by bombardment,
has been transformed into a place of hope for the hopeless,
shining like a beacon in a very dark corner of the world.

New Life after a Season of Death

The clinic and the rehabilitation centre were not the only evidence of reconstruction in Karabakh. Over time, the bombed-out Stepanakert hospital, where operations had been carried out without anaesthetic, was rebuilt. Two banks were doing business in the capital, and merchandise was once again appearing in local shops.

The village of Talysch, just two kilometres from the border, had been one of the first to be overrun by Azerbaijan's troops. Its civilians fled from enemy tanks and bombs, leaving their houses to be destroyed in the Azeri scorched-earth policy, which had left gaping stone shells beneath the skies of Karabakh. Now the village was slowly returning from the ashes.

Talysch's school building had been flattened by an incoming Azeri bomb. The 150 pupils owed their lives to their headmaster, Valeri Babayon, who heard talk of the imminent bombing raid on Azeri radio and managed to sound the warning. Stone by stone the classrooms were being rebuilt.

Even the massacred village of Maraghar gradually experienced a resurrection – in a new location. The original was still in Azeri hands. During the rebuilding process, Caroline Cox was invited to inspect the progress. She and her colleagues were given a speech of welcome by a village woman who seemed cheerful and composed. Afterwards, however, when she talked to Caroline privately, she revealed the depth of her loss and grief during the carnage. "That day I lost all four of my sons who were trying to defend the village, but they had nothing to defend it with. They managed to hold the Azeris off just long enough for some of us to escape. They all died that day, and my daughter-in-law also died, therefore I am looking after the grandchildren. We have nothing; we didn't only lose our families, we also lost all our cattle. Our children have forgotten the taste of milk."

In response to pressure from Caroline Cox, Christian

Solidarity Worldwide, an organization with which she was affiliated at the time, undertook the project of replacing the village's dairy herd. When Caroline returned later to New Maraghar she was greeted by the same woman she had met before. "Every family now has a cow," the woman reported with a smile, "and all our children now know the taste of milk."

Flashpoint in a Dangerous World

When the Iron Curtain collapsed, Baroness Cox could at last turn her attention from those who suffered under the often ruthless repression of Marxist totalitarianism. As the Soviet system crumbled, her path led her to Nagorno-Karabakh. Although the Karabakh conflict itself was not dominated by an Islamist agenda, the conflict was marked by typical jihadi tactics, including beheadings, torture, rape, mutilations of corpses, looting and burning of villages, and the kidnapping of women and children together with the recruitment of Mujahedin mercenaries in the last stages of the war. Even today, because of the rich oil resources in the region, and because of pan-Turkic aspirations, Nagorno-Karabakh remains a flashpoint in a highly combustible part of the world.

Caroline Cox's eyes light up when she speaks of the people she has come to love in Nagorno-Karabakh – courageous men and women who work as hard to rebuild their land as they did to defend it. She cherishes her friendship with the little country's military heroes, elected officials, church leaders, medical workers and ordinary citizens who, like the old farmer, know that dignity can be a crown of thorns. And Nagorno-Karabakh's people return her love. She is, in their eyes, a living saint, or, as one woman put it, "our Mother Teresa".

But Baroness Cox remains concerned about Artsakh's future. She writes of the lingering dangers:

> *New life is emerging like a phoenix from the ashes of destruction in Armenia and Karabakh. It would not only*

be a tragedy for the Armenian people if attempts were to be made to extinguish it, but it would be a calamity of grave geopolitical significance for the whole region and further afield. Armenia has the misfortune to be located not only on a geological fault line, but also on a spiritual and geopolitical fault line, which has precipitated catastrophic events with massive tolls of death, destruction and suffering. Every effort must be made to try to avert further calamities and to enable the people throughout the region to live in peace and stability, with freedom and justice for all.

The Archbishop of Nagorno-Karabakh spoke of the conflict in profound words, written at the height of the war, when 400 missiles a day were raining down on his city, his own home had been reduced to rubble, and his people were dying around him.

"The help of God is great and immeasurable when the human heart turns to Him with fervour," the Archbishop said. "Our nation has again begun to find its faith after 70 years of Communism. Our people are praying in basements, in cellars and in the field of battle, where we have to defend our land and the lives of those who are near and dear. It is not only the perpetrators of crime and evil who commit sin, but also those who stand by – seeing and knowing – and who do not condemn it or try to avert it. Blessed are the peacemakers, for they will be called sons of God. We do not hate; we believe in a God of love. We must love. Even if there are demonic forces at work, not only in this conflict, but in other parts of the world, we must still love … we must always love."

BURMA

Scale 1:32,000,000 at 5°N
Mercator Projection

0   500 Kilometers
0   500 Miles

Boundary representation is not necessarily authoritative.
Names in Vietnam are shown without diacritical marks.

CHAPTER FOUR

Burma – "Land without Evil"

It is a wet and blustery November evening in 2002. In the heart of London the House of Lords is in session, and Baroness Cox, despite a bout of flu, has shed her raincoat and umbrella and is addressing her peers. She has introduced the plight of the Burmese people to the House, and, no matter how ill she may feel, she is well aware that she speaks on behalf of a beleaguered population half a world away whose men, women and children are in far worse straits than her own.

It is hardly the first time Caroline Cox has addressed the issue of Burma, and everyone is well aware that she knows what she's talking about. In fact, she has just returned from yet another trip to South-East Asia. Now, standing before the Lords, she describes two recent defectors from the Burmese army that she has recently interviewed. Both boys were abducted at a very young age and forced to join the Burmese army, and their stories serve as a startling introduction to an almost unbelievable story.

> One boy is a young Buddhist, aged fourteen, from a town in the Yan Gon area. He had been captured by SPDC (State Peace and Development Council) soldiers when he was eleven years old. He was standing at a bus station on the way to visit his aunt, when soldiers in uniform grabbed him and took him to Ta Kyin Koe First Battalion Camp. He was not allowed to contact his parents and has not been able to get in touch with them for the past three years.
> He said there were many boys of a similar age in the

camp. After eight months he was sent to a training camp for regular soldiers of the 5th Battalion, where he underwent basic training for four to five months before being sent to Light Infantry Battalion 341 in Papun township in Karen State. After a few days he was sent to the front line. In a unit of 30 soldiers, fifteen were about his age. They were treated like soldiers, having to undertake regular military activities. They were sometimes beaten by the NCOs.

During seven or eight months at the front line, he saw villages being attacked; local villagers were rounded up and had to work for the army or pay fines to avoid such work.

The SPDC told him and the other boy soldiers that the Karen people would kill them if they ran away. He believed them, but he was so unhappy that he did escape, being prepared to die rather than remain in the army.

A Journey to the Land of Smiles

From the Iron Curtain of Marxist totalitarianism to the iron fist of militant Islam, Baroness Cox has travelled and spoken tirelessly about human rights under some of the world's most repressive regimes. But Burma's story is singular – the account of a brutal dictatorship with seemingly little ideological motivation other than a psychotic drive to cling to power, silence dissent and eradicate rivals. In the process, the Burmese people's suffering remains unrelieved, in spite of all the efforts of their heroic and forthright spokeswoman for freedom and democracy, Nobel Laureate Aung San Suu Kyi, who has been imprisoned or under house arrest almost continuously since 1988.

In November 1994, Baroness Cox was invited to Burma for the first time by Dr Martin Panter, a highly regarded English doctor who has worked for years among that nation's ethnic minorities. Burma (or Myanmar, as the ruling *junta* prefers to call it) is the size of Texas, a scenic and colourful land of mountains and rivers. It adjoins Laos and Thailand, the other corners of the Golden Triangle – one of the world's major opium-exporting centres. Burma was once known as the Land of the Golden Pagodas, one of the strongest enclaves of Theravada Buddhism in all Asia.

But Caroline Cox's mission had little to do with illicit drugs or Theravada Buddhism. Her goal was to gather facts about the Karen people, a tribal minority who were being driven out of their land by Burmese troops. The Karen were locked in a war that had been raging for years and appeared to be drawing to a bitter conclusion. Lady Cox, Dr Panter and a team of British medics had spent the night in a mission station in the town of Chiang Mai in northern Thailand. From there they would make a voyage by longboat to the refugee camps in the borderlands, and then enter Burma itself.

Many Karen converted to Christianity in the early 1800s, fought alongside the British in World War II, and faced intense persecution from 1947 when the Burmese authorities set fire to 500 Karen Christians as they worshipped in a church in Tavoy State. Today this besieged ethnic group, which makes up less than 10 per cent of Burma's population, is being systematically driven from the country's coastal region.

Their land, in Burma's eastern hills and delta, was once known as Kwathoolei, roughly translated as "land of smiles" or "land without evil". The Karen are among the earliest indigenous inhabitants of Burma, migrating from Mongolia in the centuries around the time of Christ, hundreds of years before the Myen, who would go on to dominate the region.

The Karen cherish an unusual religious heritage. From generation to generation a legend was passed down that a white man would one day arrive from a faraway land, and would reveal to the Karen the truth about the gods through the golden book that he would bring with him. Many visitors heard the legend and sought to exploit it for personal gain. But in the eighteenth century, the pioneer missionary Adoniram

Judson reached the Upper Salween district of Kwathoolei and preached – from the Holy Bible he carried with him – the truth of God revealed through the Christian faith.

"Successive authoritarian governments in Rangoon have harassed, brutalized, tortured and killed countless thousands of Karen villagers," Dr Panter explained to Caroline Cox as he briefed her about their mission. "They are liable to be murdered, raped, enslaved and pressed into forced labour." He told her of possibly thousands of Karen tribespeople who had been killed or disabled by mines, massacres and machine guns. "They are up against a terror regime," he continued. "Even if they flee to the refugee camps on the border, the conditions are severe and they may still be subject to attack. After some 46 years of fighting, these peace-loving and gentle people are weary of war."

The situation in Burma was desperate and depressing. Caroline might well have had second thoughts about her journey, considering the research she had done before leaving England and the grim picture Dr Panter now sketched out for her. But then he told her a story. If ever there was evidence that God was protecting and encouraging a mission, it could not have been more apparent than during one of his earlier journeys to Burma.

A Cloud of Protection

Dr Panter was seated at a table in a jungle area, eating a simple meal with his colleagues. On that occasion, their party included a member of the Karen intelligence, who told Dr Panter that the Burmese were planning a major offensive the following day. He had solid information that an air strike would be followed by an infantry attack. This Karen agent had picked up signals on Burmese radio suggesting that two battalions of soldiers were poised to move into the very area Dr Panter and his team were about to visit. There would be an air strike by fighter planes the following morning.

Panter faced a difficult decision. Not only was he responsible for his team, but also for his daughters, Rachel, thirteen and Juliet, nine, and his three-year-old son, Nathaniel, all of whom were with him. "I'd heard more than enough times about what the Burmese soldiers do," he explained to Caroline Cox. "Not only do they rape and kill but they torture. They also use children to walk in front of the soldiers as human minesweepers. So I knew what would happen if we were captured."

Feeling shaken by the news and realizing they were utterly dependent on God, the team gathered to pray. As they poured out their fears and questions to heaven, Martin felt drawn to Psalm 27. He looked it up in his Bible, then read it aloud: "When my enemies and my foes attack me, they will stumble and fall. Though an army besiege me, my heart will not fear; though war break out against me, even then will I be confident."

Encouraged, Dr Panter, his children and his team of eye specialists decided to go ahead with their mission. The next morning they set off in speedboats on the long boat ride, determined to continue their work unhindered. In the course of the day, although they heard the sound of fighter planes above the clouds, the threatened attack did not take place. And the medical mission was declared a success.

"It was only on my next visit to Burma", Dr Panter confided in Lady Cox, "that I found out what had actually happened."

The air strike had been scheduled to begin once the morning mist burned off, an event as dependable in that part of the world as the rising of the sun. But on that particular day, something unprecedented took place. Instead of the mists being dispersed, huge cumulus clouds began to billow up from the river until they formed a deep and impenetrable bank. Somewhere, high above, fighter bombers could be heard, circling futilely, searching for a break in the clouds. The freak weather conditions continued until the pilots' fuel ran so low that they were forced to ditch their bombs and go back to their base.

"Almost all of the bombs fell on their own troops," Panter concluded with a wry smile, "apart from one that killed two Karen chickens."

The planes had returned to Rangoon and the soldiers had withdrawn from the area.

It was an encouraging report, and it served as an affirmation for Caroline Cox that she was, indeed, in the right place. She knew a great deal about the horrific abuses in Burma. Now she had high hopes of witnessing the truth for herself.

Beautiful Nation, Tragic History

The seeds of today's nearly indescribable human rights situation in Burma/Myanmar were planted during the years that Burma spent under the authority of the British Empire, starting in the early nineteenth century. In those days England ruled India, and when several Burmese military excursions entered colonial Indian territory, the British eventually subdued Burma and recast it as a province of India – a Crown Colony.

The situation wasn't all bad. Under British rule, the Burmese enjoyed increasing success particularly in rice exports, and their economy began to flourish. However, at the same time existing ethnic tensions were exacerbated, as the British showed a preference for Indians in the administration of the country, while they placed Christian Karen people in the army. This led to protests against the British and an atmosphere of unrest.

In the 1930s, the nation was rocked by a peasant uprising followed by a student strike organized by a young man named Aung San. In 1937 Britain agreed to the separation of Burma from India and to partial self-government. Five years later, a wave of anti-British nationalism ushered in another empire: the Japanese "Empire of the Rising Sun". The Burma Independence Army, founded by Aung San, fought alongside the Japanese to drive the British out of Burma. But when Japan's promise of freedom proved false, Aung San established the Anti-Fascist People's Freedom League (AFPFL) and resorted to helping the British regain control of his country. Ultimately, the Japanese were defeated at a showdown near the Irrawaddy River.

That year, 1945, General Aung San fathered a daughter, Aung San Suu Kyi. When she was two years old, her father was assassinated on the brink of achieving his dream of an independent Burma. When Aung San died, another dream died as well – that of a federal Burmese constitution offering equal status to ethnic minorities.

On 4 January 1948, Burma was granted full independence from Britain. As the dominant Burmans sought to impose an artificial national unity on 135 disparate racial groups, the historic freedoms of those ethnic minorities was ignored. The new socialist parliamentary democracy found itself embroiled in a civil war with the Karen National Liberation Army, the Karenni, the Mon and the Communists.

A series of regimes came and went until late summer 1987 when students took to the streets of Rangoon. The following spring, workers rioted. Students demonstrating on the White Bridge across Inya Lake were beaten to death by riot police. Forty-two of them were rounded up and locked in a waiting van, where they were left to suffocate. On 8 August, the army was ordered to restore order; they began to shoot into the crowds. Across Burma, as many as 10,000 unarmed demonstrators were gunned down while an estimated 700,000 fled the country. Still, public protests and calls for democracy continued. Multi-party elections were promised within three months. But democracy was not the result. What the Burmese people got instead was a military coup.

General Saw Maung seized power on 18 September

1988. He suspended the constitution, imposed martial law and transferred authority to the Orwellian-sounding State Law and Order Restoration Council (SLORC).

The *junta* claimed it was providing a new beginning. The country's name was changed to Myanmar and its capital became Yangon. Steps were taken to liberalize the economy, even to stage democratic elections – but with an ominous twist. The leader of the opposing National League for Democracy, Aung San Suu Kyi, daughter of the late Aung San, was placed under house arrest. Nevertheless, her party won a landslide victory at the elections in May 1990, claiming 82 per cent of the parliamentary seats.

Despite the election's clear mandate, however, nothing changed. The military, whose party had gained just 10 per cent of the vote, refused to recognize the election results and arrested many of the elected politicians. Thousands of pro-democracy activists were interrogated, tortured and imprisoned. The International Committee of the Red Cross later withdrew from Burma because the government would not permit private access to prisoners.

In 1991, Aung San Suu Kyi, who had drawn her inspiration from the non-violent protests of Martin Luther King and Mahatma Gandhi, was awarded the Nobel Peace Prize. Meanwhile, a military crackdown was begun against the Christian Karen and the Muslim-led pro-independence movement. Within a year more than 100,000 Muslims were to flee the country.

In 1997, the State Law and Order Restoration Council (SLORC) was renamed the State Peace and Development Council (SPDC); the regime has been under the authority of General Than Shwe since April 1992.

By 2006, Suu Kyi had been under house arrest or imprisoned for ten of the last 16 years. After 2004 she was nearly incommunicado, although in November 2006 she was permitted a rare visit by a United Nations Under-Secretary. Major news sources reported that her spirits were strong; her health was described as good, though she was in need of regular medical care.

As for her beloved country, Freedom House's 2006 *Freedom in the World* survey reported:

> *The UN Commission on Human Rights in Geneva condemns the regime each year for committing grave human rights abuses. Annual resolutions commonly highlight a systematic pattern of extrajudicial, summary, or arbitrary executions; arrests, incommunicado detention, and "disappearances"; rape, torture, inhuman treatment, and forced labour, including the use of children; and forced relocation and the denial of freedom of assembly, association, expression, religion, and movement. Police and security forces that commit such abuses operate in a climate of impunity, as such incidents are not commonly investigated and prosecutions are rare.*
>
> *Some of the worst human rights abuses take place in the seven states dominated by ethnic minorities, who comprise approximately 35 per cent of Burma's population. In these border states, the* tatmadaw, *or Burmese armed forces, kill, beat, rape, and arbitrarily detain civilians. For example, an April 2004 report issued by the Karen Women's Organization documents numerous cases of rape committed against Karen women by members of the army as part of a strategy to intimidate, control, and shame ethnic-minority populations.*

Caroline Cox's 1994 trip with Dr Panter was only the beginning of her engagement with Burma's abused people. Her determination to bring attention to Burma's human rights violations has deepened with every passing year. She is particularly sensitive to the needs of Burma's minority populations, which suffer the most at the hands of the ruling regime.

Today, the refugee camps dotting the Thai-Burmese border are home to untold thousands who have been driven from their homes and sources of income. The camps consist of rudimentary houses on stilts, with thatched roofs and thin woven walls through which unshaded sunlight streams. There is no shortage of camps to visit and no shortage of victims to tell their stories. During her trips to Burma, Caroline Cox can be found sitting for hours, an interpreter by her side, interviewing refugees and filling up notebook after notebook. Each of her reports confirms the ones that preceded it, entailing horrible incidents of the Burmese army's systematic strategies: rape, murder, massacre, torture, mutilation, abduction of villagers – including the very elderly, alongside pregnant women and small children – who are used as slave labourers and human minesweepers.

Since that first visit, Baroness Cox has spoken about Burma in the House of Lords and at small church groups, at elite military conferences and in television interviews. She has never stopped speaking as an eyewitness to Burma's sorrows. In 2006, she reported:

> *In Karen, Karenni and Shan States there is still resistance by local armed forces and military offensives against civilians' villages, causing death and displacement on a massive scale. During the summer months of 2006, over 18,000 more Karen people had to flee their homes to live as Internally Displaced People (IDPs) in conditions of acute deprivation, hiding in the mountainous jungles, with no adequate shelter, food or medical care. In Chin and Kachin States a ceasefire was agreed, which allowed the SPDC to occupy the land, with their policies of forced labour, as well as religious persecution, intimidation and discrimination. In these predominantly Christian states, churches and crosses have been destroyed and, in many places, replaced by pagodas. The people are denied education beyond Grade 10 in their own state and in many places, especially in the areas inhabited by the Hill tribes, there is no health care. Villagers may have to walk for five days to reach a clinic but they are denied treatment if they*

*cannot pay. The peoples of these states feel they are being
subjected to a slow process of cultural genocide.*

Relentless Assaults on Burmese Minorities

Since 1996 the Burmese army has destroyed at least 2,350 villages. In addition to the over 110,000 refugees in Thailand
there are at least 1 million internally displaced people in eastern Burma, and perhaps 2 million in the whole country. Some
of these IDPs are held in 176 SPDC-controlled relocations –
more like concentration camps than places of refuge.
Hundreds of thousands more are hiding in the jungle, with little access to food, medicine or shelter and at great risk of
attack by the SPDC. When the SPDC attacks villages, its soldiers often deliberately destroy or loot medical clinics, attack
medical relief teams, and deny those taken for forced labour or
relocation access to basic medicines.

Another of the many gross violations of human rights
committed by the SPDC is the use of child soldiers. Human
Rights Watch recently published a report called *My Gun Was
As Tall As Me*, which concludes that Burma has more child soldiers than any other country in the world. Out of an estimated
350,000 troops, as many as 70,000 – 20 per cent of the military
– are children. Other relief and development agency findings
corroborate this report. Baroness Cox says, "I have spoken
with some of these child soldiers, who escaped at great risk.
Their stories are deeply disturbing. One former Burmese boy
soldier said that out of 1,750 new soldiers in a training camp,
1,000 were children; another boy said that out of 250 new
recruits, he saw 100 children; a third boy said that in his unit
of 30 soldiers, fifteen were children."

There is a pattern to the SPDC's method of forcing children to join the army. Almost all the former child soldiers Cox
interviewed had been picked off the street by Burmese soldiers
from bus stops or on their way home from school. Their parents have no way of knowing what has happened to them. The

conditions in which they are kept are brutal. Beatings are common. A boy named "Nay" was beaten several times, one time so badly that he could not walk for a week. Another boy said he had been beaten on one occasion by nine men, because he had been late for a line-up. If they are lucky, they manage to escape, though at great risk. Nay said he escaped because "I could not bear the torture any more".

In addition to the well-documented practices of forced labour and the conscription of child soldiers, the SPDC regime uses other forms of slavery including sexual slavery as a weapon of war against ethnic national groups such as the Shan, Karen and Mon people. In her 2006 book *This Immoral Trade: Slavery in the 21st Century*, written with Dr John Marks, Baroness Caroline Cox wrote:

> *Sexual exploitation, humiliation and the systematic use of rape as a weapon of war are… well and widely documented… Despite numerous reports by… various human rights organizations, the SPDC continues to subject its citizens to these practices with impunity. Although the SPDC has been subjected to pressure by some members of the international community, the suffering of the people continues unabated – and is even escalating in scale and intensity.*

All the ethnic minority groups are vulnerable to abuse at the hands of the SPDC, including military sexual abuse. A report entitled "License to Rape: The Burmese Military Regime's Use of Sexual Violence in the Ongoing War in Shan State", cited in *This Immoral Trade*, typifies the level of violence reported across the spectrum of ethnic national groups. Caroline Cox and John Marks write:

> *… rape is officially condoned as a "weapon of war" against the civilian populations. There appears to be a concerted strategy by the Burmese army troops to rape Shan women as part of their anti-insurgency activities. The incidents described [in "License to Rape"] were committed by*

soldiers from 52 different battalions. 83% of the rapes were committed by officers, usually in front of their own troops. The rapes involved extreme brutality and often torture such as beating, mutilation and suffocation. 25% of the rapes resulted in death, in some incidences with bodies being deliberately displayed to local communities. 61% were gang rapes; women were raped within military bases, and in some cases they were detained and raped repeatedly for periods of up to four months. Out of the total 173 documented incidents, in only one case was a perpetrator punished by his commanding officer. More commonly, the complainants were fined, detained, tortured and even killed by the military.

In addition to policies of physical violence against the ethnic minorities, verging on ethnic cleansing, there is the policy of so-called "Burmanization" or "cultural genocide". The plight of the Chin is one example of this. One Chin leader told the Baroness that when he was at school he had been taught his own language, but now the Chin language has been removed from the school curriculum. It is illegal to publish a Chin-language Bible, even though the Chin are 90% Christian. Even Burmese-language Bibles cannot be freely circulated in Chin state.

"Religious persecution happens on a daily basis," a Chin leader told Caroline Cox. In every major Chin town or village it has long been a community practice for the Chin to erect a Christian cross. But the SPDC has destroyed most of these crosses and replaced them with statues of Buddha. Fertile land farmed by the Chin has often been confiscated and given to ethnic Burmese. "It is a systematic campaign by the SPDC," the Chin representative told Cox. "When people lose their culture and traditions, they lose what they are campaigning for."

The Karenni

The Karenni, who make up a tiny minority of the Burmese population, have been fighting for their existence since 1948, when the Burmese army marched into their capital, Loikaw, to occupy their territory from then on. Still today they battle for their survival. Tens of thousands have been displaced. As with the other Burmese minorities, many have fled the country, while the rest languish in refugee camps or live in illegal settlements, hidden in the dense tropical forests.

It is difficult to report exact numbers, but there are approximately 300,000 Karenni people, of whom 250,000 remain inside their homeland while the rest have fled across the border into Thailand. The majority of the villages (approximately 100) in Shadaw region and about 100 villages around Mawchi have reportedly been destroyed by SPDC troops. There are many thousands of Karenni villagers living as IDPs in very harsh conditions, trying to survive in the jungle. They can usually return to their villages only on a temporary basis, because it is not safe to stay there. One particular danger is that of land mines planted by SPDC troops.

People do not want to leave their land, despite the hardships and deprivation they experience in trying to stay. Eventually the situation becomes intolerable. As there is no health care in many places, or it is available only at a prohibitive cost, and with no NGOs allowed into the region, many people die. There are no schools for most displaced people, and if they do exist the fees are exorbitant. If parents manage to raise the money for school fees, they must also pay for textbooks, which they can little afford. Many children are thus denied even a basic education.

The Chin People

Meanwhile, on the border of India and Burma, another minority group – primarily Christian – also faces forced labour, torture and religious persecution in Chin State. In March 2006, along with a delegation from the Humanitarian Aid Relief Trust (HART), Christian Solidarity Worldwide (CSW) and the Norwegian Mission to the East (NME), Baroness Cox visited the Chin people. Extensive eyewitness accounts of prison labour conditions describe shackled prisoners working on road-construction projects, rubber plantations and tea plantations in Chin State and other parts of Burma. An eyewitness told the delegation that prisoners in one labour camp are yoked like oxen and forced to plough the fields.

In the delegation's report, the horrific treatment of imprisoned Chin people is described categorically and in detail:

> Food: *Standard food rations for one meal may consist of a spoon of boiled rice mixed with wild banana leaf and sweet potato leaf. Prisoners are so hungry that they eat their guards' pig swill on the way to work. If caught doing this, they are severely beaten. Some prisoners reportedly eat their own faeces.*

> Sleep deprivation: *In some (at least four) camps, each prisoner had an empty milk can attached to the end of his bunk. Every night, he was required to wake up every fifteen minutes, to strike the can and to shout his personal number in order to prove he had not escaped.*

> Physical maltreatment: *Prisoners are constantly chained with leg irons attached to an iron belt. If they can bribe the jailer, they will be given lightweight chains; if not, they have to suffer the constant discomfort of heavy chains. The constant chafing causes lacerations which become swollen, inflamed and, in some instances, infected.*

> Clothing: *Their only garments are a thin shirt and "longyi" (sarong). Those who work in paddy fields are bitten by water leeches; all suffer cuts and bruising from being beaten by jailers. All the lacerations caused by the chains, the bites*

and the beatings cause localized and systemic infections. As they are not given any medical treatment, many die.

Work: *Prisoners have to work from 6am to 6pm without a rest, except for their meal break. Even those who are sick or blind have to work. Many die of exhaustion, disease and malnutrition.*

Measures to deter escape attempts: *The camps have relatively few guards, so in order to prevent prisoners from attempting to escape, harsh punishments are imposed, sometimes resulting in death. Anyone caught trying to escape may be subjected to horrendous torture: some have their hands tied behind their back and are dragged along the ground "like a dead animal"; others are laid out on the ground, bound hand and foot. Others have had burning bamboo placed alongside them so that they are slowly "roasted". If they scream because of the pain, a heated crowbar is used to pierce their flesh until the bone is exposed. It takes two to three days for the victim to die.*

Why Such Brutality?

In 1992 the French petroleum corporation Total, along with its US partner Unocal, signed a billion-dollar natural-gas deal in the form of a "Memorandum of Understanding". They began work in 1996 on a pipeline to carry natural gas from an offshore field in the Andaman Sea to a new power station 270 kilometres inside Thailand. The controversial deal promised to provide an annual income for the Burma regime of between $200 and $400 million. (Dominic Fauldner, "In the Name of Money", *Asiaweek*, 9 May 1997; also *Covert Action Quarterly*, autumn 1996.)

The preparation for the actual construction of the pipeline resulted in the forced relocation of up to 30,000 villages in the Karen and Mon territories. Many of the villagers, it has been reported, were forced to burn their own homes and clear their own land. ("Human Rights and Progress Towards Democracy in Burma", The Parliament of the Commonwealth of Australia, Joint Standing Committee on Foreign Affairs, Defence and Trade, October 1996, p. 32; also International Labour Organization.) Unocal claimed to have visited the area and found no evidence of abuses of human rights. Meanwhile, Total's website denies that villages were destroyed or that forced labour was used in the pipeline's construction. [http://burma.total.com/en/gazier/p_2_2.htm]

The UN Special Rapporteur, however, has cited "numerous reports from a wide variety of sources" that state that forced labour was in fact employed to build "road [and] railway bridges and gas pipelines". ("Situation on Human Rights in Myanmar", *United Nations*, 8 October 1996, paragraph 132.) Meanwhile, the National League for Democracy claimed to have extensive evidence of slave labour along the route of the pipeline. According to the US oil company Unocal, this claim was a "fabrication".

Besides Burma/Myanmar, the country that stands to profit most from the pipeline is Thailand, for whom the gas is intended and whose policies toward the refugees remain under scrutiny. In 1993, the *Bangkok Nation* (quoted in the *New Internationalist*) accused Thailand of burning down two refugee camps for reasons "probably related to the gas pipeline". Dr Martin Panter, in co-operation with Christian Solidarity International, believes that the burning may have been encouraged or even orchestrated by the Thai government for economic reasons, to compel Karen refugees to return to the territories they had fled from in Burma. Nearly 8,000 refugees were left without shelter after two fires razed their refugee camps in 1997.

Dr Panter repeatedly tried to investigate the fires and also accusations that the Thai military had been shelling refugees, executing several who refused to leave the area. As a result, his access to refugee camps was barred. Later, the Thai commander-in-chief said at a press conference, "Thailand has a legitimate right to protect the country against intruders. In this case we had the right to destroy them."

When Dr Panter finally managed to get through to Karen refugees at another camp, he was presented with a painting by a nine-year-old boy. The child had drawn his village in Burma. It was in flames, and his family was attempting to cross the river Moei into Thailand with all their belongings. "As they cross," says Dr Panter, describing the boy's artwork, "Thai solders with fixed bayonets point their weapons at them."

A Corner of the Golden Triangle

Aside from fossil fuels, there is even bigger money to be made in the Golden Triangle – Burma, Thailand and Laos – the world's number-one supplier of heroin. Its fields of opium poppies are believed to produce more than 50 per cent of the global market – enough to satisfy the USA's addiction many times over.

According to the Karen National Union, peace talks with the Myanmar regime broke down when the Karen refused to assist the regime in the heroin trade. It is generally understood that this trade has distribution networks transporting the drugs into China, Taiwan, Singapore, India, Bangladesh, Nepal, the United States and Australia. It is widely reported that Burma's drug trade exploded in the early twenty-first century, due largely to internal chaos and corrupt law enforcement.

Scholar, journalist and human rights campaigner Benedict Rogers discusses the "why" of Burma's agony in his powerful book *A Land Without Evil*. "What is it that causes a regime, even one that is intolerant of democracy and dissent, to behave so brutally?"

He continues:

How is it that tatmadaw *soldiers can find the will to tie eight-year-old children to a tree and use them for target practice, or put a baby in a rice-pounder and crush it to death? What threats do those children, or that baby, pose them? How is it that soldiers do not stop at their ordinary military duty – shooting – which in itself is bad but is what all armies do? But instead, they denigrate their opponents in the most barbaric ways. Go Nai, for example, was attacked at 8 pm on 11 September, 1994 when Burma Army troops entered his village. They cut his nose off, gouged his eyes out, stabbed his ears while he was still alive, and then finished him off with a knife to his chest. Why?*

(CSI Report, "Visit to the Thai-Burmese Border",
December 7 –13, 1996)

It is difficult if not impossible to truly understand, and therefore to answer the questions "why?" One can put it down to the old adage that "power corrupts and absolute power corrupts absolutely", but Daw Aung San Suu Kyi believes that is not quite true. "It is not power that corrupts but fear," she has written. "Fear of losing power corrupts those who wield it, and fear of the scourge of power corrupts those who are subject to it."

(From Suu Kyi's essay to commemorate her receiving the 1990
Sakharov Prize for Freedom of Thought

Burma: Bombs into Bells

Caroline Cox has spent invaluable time in Burma, both among the suffering displaced people and in the refugee camps across the border in Thailand. She describes her impressions.

I will never forget walking through one camp soon after it had suffered a raid, feeling darkness like that of the black-ened landscape around me: huts burnt, everything destroyed. We entered the remains of a hut and encoun-tered what I can only call a miracle of grace. *Ma Su, a 38-year-old Karen lady whose home was destroyed by*

*shelling, was also shot by a soldier running rampage
through the camp. She is recovering from her wounds, but
still in pain. When we asked her what she felt about the
soldier who shot her so gratuitously, her reply was both
simple and wholehearted:*

"I love him. The Bible tells us to love our enemies
– so of course I love him: he is my brother."

*What a glorious example of Christ's redeeming love
which can transform brutality and suffering into redemp-
tive, forgiving love.*

*I will never forget another occasion when we had
walked across the border into Burma, and climbed up a
steep mountain to meet some of the internally displaced
people (IDPs is the jargon phrase) living in primitive conditions in constant fear of bombardment. Their little camp
had been bombed three times in the last few months. As
we approached them, feeling totally inadequate to begin to
address the enormity of their needs, they came running to
us with tears in their eyes, crying:*

"Thank God you have come. We thought the world
had forgotten us. But the fact that you are here makes all
the difference: to know that we are not forgotten gives us
the strength to continue to struggle to survive. It wouldn't
matter if you brought nothing with you – the fact that you
are here is all that matters."

*On our way down the mountain from our
encounter with this besieged, bombarded and vulnerable
little Karen community, we suddenly heard a sound which
resembled that of a church bell. Intrigued, we followed the
sound and found a little worshipping Baptist church. We
also found that the bell which had summoned us was a
Burmese bombshell, lovingly transformed into a single
chime. I thought to myself,* in today's world, instead of
swords into ploughshares, we have bombs into bells.

*The bombs continue to fall on innocent civilians –
Christian, Buddhist, animist and Muslim. Please pray*

that soon there will be a political solution in favour of democracy, that the bombs will cease, and that the church bells will ring in celebration for peace with justice for all the people of Burma.

Pastor Simon

In her book *Cox's Book of Modern Saints and Martyrs*, Baroness Cox writes about a man for whom she has deep admiration – a Christian who goes by the name of Pastor Simon. He is a Karen who fled for his life from Burma and continues to serve God and his countrymen from a refugee camp in Thailand. She writes, "To anyone else, Pastor Simon's circumstances are bleak, but he has transformed the deprivations of life in a camp for the displaced from a situation of despair into a place of hope. He has established a theological seminary in the camps and cares for many Karen children, including orphans who have had to flee from their homes in Burma in order to survive. Pastor Simon's perspective on the troubles around him is both humbling and heartbreaking.

> *"They call us a displaced people,*
> *But praise God, we are not misplaced.*
> *They say they see no hope for our future,*
> *But praise God, our future is as bright as the promises of God.*
> *They say the life of our people is a misery,*
> *But praise God, our life is a mystery.*
> *For what they say is what they see,*
> *And what they see is temporal.*
> *But ours is the eternal.*
> *All because we put ourselves,*
> *In the hands of God we trust."*

INDONESIA

Scale 1:32,000,000 at 5°N

Mercator Projection

0   500 Kilometers

0   500 Miles

dary representation is not necessarily authoritative.
es in Vietnam are shown without diacritical marks.

CHAPTER FIVE

Indonesia – Martyrs and Miracles

Basking alongside lapis and turquoise seas, lazing beside coral reefs teeming with undersea life, Indonesia's beautiful Spice Islands – otherwise known as the Moluccas – were once a haven for tourists. Honeymooners, day trippers and holiday-makers flocked to idyllic beaches and exotic destinations where sun, sand and the gentle sound of the sea provided a welcome respite from the hectic pace of Western cities.

These islands, located in the world's largest Muslim nation, also served as an inspiring example of religious toler-ance, for Muslims and Christians had lived peaceably together there for centuries. But since January 1999, the paradise of the Moluccas has been transformed into a tragic nightmare. In less than a decade, thousands of people have been killed in religious conflicts, and tens of thousands forced to hide in dense jungles, living as internally displaced peoples in condi-tions so harsh that the fragile and frail could not survive.

Indonesia has a population of over 200 million, of which around 88 per cent are Muslims and only about 8 per cent are Christians (5 per cent Protestant, 3 per cent Roman Catholic). However, in the Moluccas there is a sizeable Christian com-munity, representing about 50 per cent of the local population. Tensions between Christians and Muslims have increased in recent years, since Indonesian government policy encouraged internal migration into the Moluccas, causing competition for jobs and resources. But the tension suddenly exploded into violence in 1999 with ceaseless pressure in Sulawesi, which is

believed by local people to have been instigated and exacerbated by outsiders.

Caroline Cox first visited Indonesia in April 2000. As she
flew into Ambon, the Moluccas' largest city, she was amazed
by the area's breathtaking scenery: high mountains covered
with forests and lush vegetation; beautiful coastlines, with
high cliffs cascading into deep azure-blue seas. "But as we
drove from the airport," she recalls, "the scenes of man's
destructiveness obliterated the beauty: we saw blackened villages, ruined homes, and burnt-out churches and mosques
that testified to bitter intercommunal fighting."

Local Indonesians have told Lady Cox during her
numerous visits how deeply they regret the conflict. Some
Muslims and Christians described instances in which they've
tried to protect each other's communities, and in some cases at
the cost of innocent lives. But, subsequently, many hundreds
of jihad warriors, operating under such names as Laskar Jihad
and Jemaah Islamiyah, have converged on Ambon and other
locations such as Palu and Poso in Sulawesi. Most come originally from other parts of Indonesia or other countries. And
the results, at times, have been horrifying, as Caroline Cox has
described to audiences around the world.

> *A young Christian boy from Indonesia told us what hap-
> pened to him and his friends at a Sunday School Bible
> Study Camp. The children were having a happy time when
> suddenly a group of jihad warriors appeared, armed with
> knives and machetes. The children ran for their lives, fol-
> lowed by the warriors. As the children hid, the warriors
> asked local Muslim farmers where the Christian children
> were hiding. The farmers replied that they had seen no
> children. Then the warriors saw the foliage move and
> exclaimed: "There are the Christian children!"*
>
> *The farmers intercepted them, claiming that it was
> the goats who were in the foliage, protecting the Christian
> children's lives. That night the children returned to camp
> to find their camp destroyed, but their resourceful teacher*

located an empty building where they all spent the night. The children were frightened, but comforted by their teacher's words of encouragement.

The next morning the jihad warriors came back, broke into the building and slaughtered the teacher in front of the children. They then challenged the children, daring them to admit that they were Christians. The children all stood firm. Then they took this boy's best friend, wrapped the Sunday School flag around him and asked who he was.

The boy replied: "I am one of Christ's soldiers."

A warrior hacked off the child's left arm with a machete.

Again the jihad leader asked: "Who do you say you are?"

Again the boy replied: "I am one of Christ's soldiers."

The killers sliced off his other arm. The mutilated boy was asked a third time: "And who do you now say you are?"

Rapidly losing strength but still conscious, the boy looked up at the jihad warrior and, and using the courtesy title appropriate for speaking to an older man, he asked, "Uncle, what do you want me to say?"

The terrorist replied: "I don't want to harm you, but because you said you are one of Christ's soldiers, I have to kill you."

With his machete he disembowelled the dying boy.

Meanwhile, the other boy, who witnessed his friend's martyrdom, shows no sign of bitterness or grief on his face. He simply demonstrates an open, innocent acceptance of the price of faith. I was reminded of these words by T.S. Eliot:

We thank Thee for Thy mercies of blood.
For the blood of Thy martyrs and saints shall enrich the earth, shall create the holy places.

> *For wherever a saint has dwelt, wherever a martyr has given his blood for the blood of Christ, There is holy ground, and the sanctity shall not depart from it…*

A Nation with Formidable Problems

Indonesia is a vast archipelago, encompassing 17,508 islands, and holding enormous potential for prosperity. It boasts abundant natural resources, a rich cultural tradition, and some of the most enticing scenery in the world. The Indonesian people are famous for their hospitality and gracious generosity. And their system of parliamentary democracy has withstood numerous challenges, while maintaining an encouraging level of economic development.

However, militant extremists first began to arrive in significant numbers in the spring of 2000; it is impossible to give precise figures but it is believed that they may have numbered 3–4,000 at the height of the conflict in the Moluccas. Their leader claims 7,000. Many more are also known to be in Sulawesi. They receive international support in the form of financial resources and personnel from countries such as Saudi Arabia, Pakistan, Afghanistan, Yemen and other Middle Eastern countries. They have set up training camps in the Moluccas and in Sulawesi.

One of their terrorist camps on the outskirts of Ambon was, for a time, clearly visible and appeared well established. Baroness Cox was told during her travels that several such camps are mobile, so that if they are approached by government security forces they are able to relocate quickly, a relatively easy and undetectable operation in the dense jungle and mountain terrain.

Indonesia's religious conflict, in which Muslim, Christian and Hindu communities have suffered, has resulted not only in death and displacement, but also in the widespread destruction of homes, places of worship, schools and hospitals. To make matters worse, its psychological scars have left communities divided by fear and intimidation. Regions that were once prosperous and beautiful have been reduced to a state of utter devastation.

Although it is primarily the Muslim and Christian communities who have been involved in the violence and who are suffering the aftermath, other communities have also suffered. On one fact-finding trip to Sulawesi, Caroline Cox visited a Hindu community, whose population, originally from Bali, had settled near Poso. An official in the Mayor's office informed her of the systematic destruction of Hindu temples. He claimed that over 40 have been destroyed.

Throughout Indonesia, people from all walks of life have expressed concern to Lady Cox that the country is soon to become a new base for the training and support of international terrorists, some with al-Qaeda connections. Some leaders even suggested that, since Afghanistan can no longer serve as a primary jihadist centre, Indonesia is an ideal alternative, with its island terrain of jungles and mountains. A population with mixed ethnic backgrounds enables incoming jihad warriors from the Middle East to be easily absorbed.

These concerns were underlined in a report, from which excerpts are shown here, that Caroline Cox wrote after one visit to Indonesia:

> *Our inbound flight to Ambon was delayed by several hours because a bomb had been found hidden in the airport at Ambon. A few days previously, the airport had been attacked by several hundred Laskar Jihad militants who had approached from three directions with a clear intention of trying to take over the airport. They were repulsed by military forces based at the airport but only after they managed to get within 50 metres of the main building.*
>
> *On the plane on which we travelled, we noticed six men whom we immediately perceived as likely to be mujahedin going to join the Laskar Jihad forces. Our suppositions were proved correct when the local newspaper in Ambon the following day reported the arrival of seven*

Afghan veterans who had just arrived to join the Laskar
Jihad forces. We were surprised to see that they were wel-
comed with delight by a small group of local police who
treated them as VIPs and escorted them from the airport
without any customs or security clearance.

Caroline Cox and her colleagues were later given information
regarding the Islamists' proposed agenda in Sulawesi: after
taking control of Poso, they had intended to continue their
military offensives against other areas with significant
Christian populations, finishing in Taraja region. Having
killed, converted or evicted the Christians, they would achieve
a demographic change, with predominantly Muslim populations. They would then be able to apply for the right to implement Shari'a (Islamic) law in these areas. Such a development
would be hard to reverse and would have far-reaching implications

A Big Problem, a Small Miracle

As has become her habit when faced with horrifying realities
around the world, Caroline Cox tries to balance them with her
Christian faith. She has often found encouragement in appar-
ent "divine interventions" that serve to reassure her that she is,
in fact, doing the right thing in the right place at the right time.
Events that seem like miracles are encouraging and inspiring.
During a church presentation, she introduces one such event:
"Please meet Berty," she smiles, as a young man's pleasant
Asian face appears on the screen. She is speaking to a group
that has assembled to hear about the plight of Indonesia's
Christians.

   She goes on to explain that Berty comes from a village
that has recently been attacked by a group of Islamist extremists. The whole community fled into the jungle, where they hid,
in terror, living in harsh conditions. After about six months in
exile, Berty grew impatient. He announced that he was not
going to allow a war to interrupt his education. So off he went,

alone, walking for several days through the jungle to find a safe village where he could go to school.

Yet despite his determination to continue his studies, Berty could not stop thinking about his friends and family, still trapped in the jungle. He somehow contacted government authorities and pleaded with them to rescue his family and the other villagers. Eventually a rescue team was assembled. They were willing to take on the task at hand, but it would cost a lot of money: £6,000 to be exact. Somehow word of this need came to the organization with whom Caroline Cox had been working. She continues:

> *Back in London, I was unaware of these developments. But on that same morning, I was due to attend a Trustees' meeting of a charitable organization. I am not paid by them, but I do have the privilege of nominating certain good causes as my personal recommendations for a certain sum each year. At the end of the meeting, Bruce, the administrator, advised me I had not spent my annual allocation. "You'd better use it as soon as possible," he warned me, "since it will no longer be available after this fiscal year."*
>
> *I was certain I had spent my allowance and was honest enough to say so. I even enumerated the details. But Bruce was adamant and I suddenly thought, "If we have a Divine Accountant and He wishes to cook the books, who am I to argue?"*
>
> *Bruce reaffirmed that I had £6,000 outstanding.*
>
> *I did not immediately know how best to use it. But just as soon as I could switch on my mobile, I heard an urgent message telling me about the possibility of rescuing the displaced Indonesian community that was trapped in a jungle.*
>
> *The report concluded that the rescue operation would cost £6,000 but they didn't have the money.*
>
> *Amazed by the precise accuracy of divine provision, I replied that I thought I just might know where I could*

find the £6,000. I phoned the Trust immediately. By that
afternoon the good news had sped to Indonesia. I visited
the island of Seram three weeks later, and arrived just as
the rescue team brought Berty's community to safety. We
had the privilege of seeing that ecstatic young man
reunited with his family – there he was embracing them
for the first time in a year. His happy face was like an elec-
tric light bulb – he couldn't stop smiling for days!

Seeking Reconciliation between Christians and Muslims

Despite the violence and conflict, as Caroline Cox has travelled around Indonesia, the traditional leaders of both the Muslim and Christian communities have repeatedly expressed a sincere wish for reconciliation and a return to normal life. They believe this is feasible, given the history of good relations between the two communities, so characteristic of the region.

Former President of Indonesia Abdurrahman Wahid has frequently affirmed his commitment to religious tolerance and cultural diversity. He has also emphasized a desire to promote peace and prevent conflict throughout Indonesia, and, as honorary president of the International Islamic Christian Organization for Reconciliation and Reconstruction (IICORR), he has expressed his support of the organization's objectives, which are:

- Provision of humanitarian assistance to those suffering from sectarian conflict;
- Encouragement of the voice of moderation and cooperation in both communities;
- Promotion of positive relationships between the Muslim and Christian communities and reconciliation in conflict areas;
- Assistance in the reconstruction of the social infrastructure, including the rebuilding of places of

Caroline's father, Robert John McNeill Love, a well-regarded surgeon and author.

Baroness Cox of Queensbury.

Caroline's father served in the Royal Army Medical Corps during World War I and as a civilian surgeon during World War II. This photograph, taken in Mesopotamia, shows tents used to isolate patients he was treating for bubonic plague.

NAGORNO KARABAKH

Happy day!

Caroline receives an award from the Government of Karabakh for humanitarian services – it is Karabakh's highest honour.

With other medal winners: Aslan Grigorian (right) the Head of Civil Defense and Mountain Rescue and Dr Gerayer Kotcharian, an academic from the Institute for Threatened Peoples, Berlin, who travelled many times with Caroline to Karabakh during the war.

BURMA

Caroline, in 1998, pictured riding an elephant belonging to General Bo Mia, Commander in Chief of the Karen National Union Army. The Karen people are a hill tribe from the eastern border region of Burma and reside primarily in Karen State.

Swaleen River, Thai-Burma border: Illegal crossing into Burma, April 1998.

Crossing into Karen State, with General Bo Mia, 1998.

A camp for displaced Karen people in the aftermath of an attack by SPDC troops.

The SPDC (State Peace and Development Council) is the official name of the military regime of Burma. In 1990, instead of honouring the electoral process, it seized power by force.

Ma Su, a Karen lady shot by SPDC soldiers. When asked what she felt about the soldier who shot her, she replied: "I love him. The Bible says we must love our enemies, so of course I love him. He is my brother."

A Karen refugee camp where a Burmese bombshell is used as a church bell – the modern version of turning "swords into ploughshares".

With Karen children in a camp for displaced people, Thai-Burma border, 1998.

INDONESIA

"Storm clouds gathering over Paradise."

Evening in Poso, Sulawesi, an epicentre of conflict where the militant Islamist group, Lasker Jihad, attacked Christian and Hindu communities.

Ambon, Southern Maluku (Spice Islands): A school teacher among the ruins of her school, destroyed by Lasker Jihad.

Children among ruins in Ambon.

The remains of Silo Church, Ambon, burnt by Lasker Jihad warriors.

Caroline with Joanna Chellapermal of Christian Solidarity Worldwide (CSW) in front of the ruins of Silo church.

EAST TIMOR

A camp for displaced peoples in Dili, 2006.

HART (Humanitarian Aid Relief Trust), was founded by Baroness Cox, to relieve suffering and sow the seeds of longer-term solutions.

This photograph shows names being called as HART aid is distributed.

NIGERIA

The Rt Rev. Zakka Lalle Nyam, the Anglican Bishop of Kano, standing in what remains of a church destroyed by jihadis (Islamic militants), June 2006.

Another Anglican church destroyed during riots in Kano.

Childen in a village destroyed by jihadis in Bauchi State, Northern Nigeria.

Cars that had been taken to a police station for safe keeping – the police fled when they were attacked.

Eye-witness to destruction: In the ruins of a Christian centre, Jos, plateau State.

SUDAN

Treating an epidemic of whooping cough, Udir, Eastern Upper Nile.

A young boy sits in the remains of a church that was destroyed during the war in Southern Sudan.

Caroline's arrival at a remote air strip in Southern Sudan.

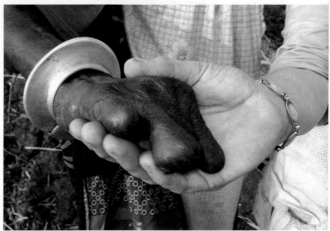

Holding the hand of a leper in Eastern Upper Nile, Sudan 2007.

A young boy from the Beja Muslim people. They had been driven by the Government of Sudan into the desert in Eastern Sudan.

Cry Freedom! A group of women and children who had just been rescued from slavery.

A family in Bahr-El-Ghazal: The mother refused to go to a Government of Sudan clinic as this would have required conversion to Islam, saying: "We are Christians and we would rather die as Christians than give up our faith."

NORTHERN UGANDA

Caroline with a fellow nurse at a Rehabilitation Centre for children who had been abducted by the Lord's Resistance Army (LRA), Feb 2006.

Children in a camp for Internally Displaced People (IDPs), near Kitgum, Northern Uganda, Feb 2006.

In the dry season, huts easily ignite causing loss of "home" and all meagre belongings.

A vehicle destroyed in an LRA attack, Feb 2006.

Conditions in camp: A five-hour wait for water, Patongo, Pader District, Feb 2006.

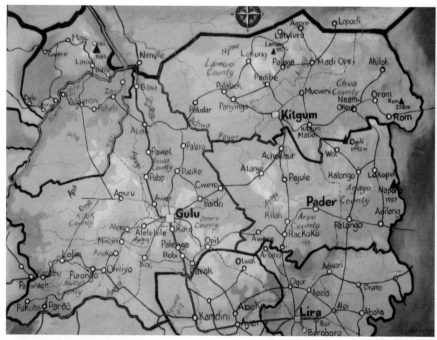

Map of Northern Uganda.

worship, schools, homes, hospitals and community
centres;

- Facilitation of settlement of persons who have been
displaced from their communities;
- Provision of educational materials to promote understanding of the beliefs, values and practices of other
faiths.

In 2004, the British government funded an interfaith delegation, and invited Protestant, Catholic and Muslim local leaders
from the Moluccas to gather in Britain. There they developed
principles of reconciliation and reconstruction, and sought out
the best ways of putting them into practice. After their return
home, when incipient conflict began to erupt again, it was
quickly and efficiently controlled. This was due to the good
faith and the plans that had been developed during the group's
time in Britain, away from the conflict area. Caroline Cox says,
"My IICORR colleagues and I hope that such initiatives may be
able to develop in other conflict areas, where local people wish
to pursue peace and to normalize relationships between previously friendly communities."

While pursuing these goals, Lady Cox, interviewed both
Christians and Muslims in several troubled areas. Many of
them emphasized that these religious groups had long lived
peacefully together as brothers and sisters and they did not
want to fight each other. One Muslim community leader
assured her that reconciliation came naturally because everyone wanted peace for economic reasons. When fighting
erupted it was impossible to organize markets, to buy or sell
produce, or to earn money. Problems caused by lack of food,
medicine and other essential supplies had therefore forced the
local people to find a solution by joining together to restore a
traditional market.

This leader informed Cox that in some regions, if
Muslims chose to go to school in a Christian area, Christians
had accompanied them and protected them. He claimed that

all the people in the area wanted peace but they needed the help of external mediators.

"I hope," he said, "that such personnel will be provided by the government."

"Christians Forced into Islamic Faith"

But there have been numerous other stories, both disturbing and frightening. One group of Christians told Caroline Cox that, when their village was attacked in early 2000, they fled into the jungle, where they hid for two weeks. On 17 January, three of them went back to their village to try to find food. They were picking fruit on their own land around the village when some Muslims confronted them.

These Muslims encouraged the Christians to come to Polin, their village, and assured them that they would not be harmed. "We only want to help you," one of the local Muslims promised. "We won't put any pressure on you to adopt our faith; we'll allow you to keep your faith; and we will keep ours."

The relieved Christians took them at their word and went with them to their village. However, after three days local people began to warn them that, if they did not convert to Islam, they would be killed – not by them, but by other Muslims from a nearby community. The Christians were so afraid they agreed to convert. When they did so, they were given Muslim names. They were also forcibly circumcised – men and women alike.

The male circumcisions were carried out by one of the local imam's assistants. The instrument in his hand was neither clean nor sharp; it was a traditional knife and was put to use with both men and women. The men suffered agonizing wounds. Two of the women were so frightened that they screamed in terror and pleaded not to be cut. Some compassion was shown to them and the knife was only passed over them without any incision, symbolizing a ritual circumcision. All the other women, however, were subjected to brutal and humiliating female genital mutilation without anaesthesia. No hygienic measures were taken, and one elderly woman died shortly afterwards.

In spite of all this, 20 traumatized families still chose to remain in Polin because they were so afraid of being killed if they tried to escape. They said they had already suffered too much and were terrified of being captured and further abused if they tried to flee. They therefore resigned themselves to living as Muslims. They were threatened that if they did not go to the mosque regularly to pray, this would be reported to the Laskar Jihad militants. The jihadists' brutal tactics of torture and mutilation were well known to all.

Another example also illustrates these aspects of contemporary military jihad in Indonesia, as reported in *The 'West', Islam and Islamism*, by Caroline Cox and John Marx, in an interview with a young man (whose name must be withheld) aged 17, from Lata-Lata island, in Bacan Group, North Maluku:

> *In February 2000, my village (I was fifteen years old) was attacked. The assault was unexpected, as our people had had no problems with Muslims. Just before it happened, one person warned us but we didn't believe him; we thought it was a provocation, so we continued fishing in the sea and working in our fields.*
>
> *At 1pm, two ships arrived and shouted that in a moment they would land and wipe us out, so we then alerted everyone we could. But the people could not prepare to defend themselves as we had no weapons.*
>
> *At 3pm the attack began. Apart from those coming from the boats (there were about a hundred men in each of the bigger boats and several smaller boats with about ten people in each) many others came from the jungle, over the mountains – it seemed as if they were about 5,000 (but it is impossible to tell). The men who came in the boats wore long white gowns; those from the jungle wore short white tunics.*
>
> *They began bombing from the jungle and shooting*

from the boats. There were about 1,700 people in our community and we had nothing to defend ourselves with. We were overwhelmed. About 70 of our people were killed. There was nothing we could do, so those who were killed were those who could not run – mainly the elderly, women and children. I saw that one of my cousins, aged seven, had been beheaded.

Another villager described how someone had been impaled on a pole and how, as the attack developed, and as we fled, he saw military men wearing white gowns, shooting his uncle, pouring fuel over him and setting him alight.

At 5pm, with the head of the village, we fled inland. By then, there was no one alive in the village. The head of the village took me with him. We walked for about an hour and then sat and prayed for God's protection. When the Laskar Jihad had attacked the village they had kept shouting: "Why do you Christians believe in Christ? Why believe in that long-haired man?"

As we were running, they had shouted, "Kill the head of the village and the pastor. They are provocateurs and terrorists. We must kill them."

We hid in the jungle. All we had to eat were coconuts and plants. Water was such a problem that people drank from muddy puddles.

Next morning, we looked at the village and saw what had happened to our families. We were very confused and didn't know what to do. It is a small island and our boats had been destroyed. Everything had been destroyed. We didn't know where to go. We had nowhere to escape. We started to bury the dead, but at 7am the Laskar Jihad returned, shouting: "Why touch those heathen?"

We realized we couldn't escape from the island and we knew that if we were caught we would be asked, "Do you want to surrender by religion (convert to Islam) or by war (be killed)?"

They sent messengers to the villagers still hiding in the jungle, saying that if the pastor did not surrender himself within three days, they would go through the island and kill everyone on the island. They also gave orders that everyone in hiding must come out and surrender or they would be hunted down and killed.

Those of us in my group in the jungle talked and agreed we would convert to Islam with our bodies – otherwise we would all be killed. But in our hearts we would not convert. When we came out of the jungle, we found that others who had already surrendered had been circumcised, including the women and girls from the age of seven.

When I was asked by the military men why I had run away, I said I believed in Christ. They said: "Christianity is not a true religion. Why do you just sing and laugh and not bow down before God?"

I could do nothing except obey them. I was also circumcised.

I saw them capture the pastor (Pastor Patissina) on Goji beach. They bound his hands and feet tightly together. He said he was thirsty and one Laskar Jihad soldier (named Baha from Bokimaki) retorted, "We are going to leave you like this until you die."

The boy was later told that the warriors eventually shot the pastor and took his body to another island, where it was hung up on public display. Also, four elders of the church had been tortured and killed alongside the pastor – their fingernails and toenails had been pulled out and their bodies hacked to pieces by machetes. Only mangled remains were found.

Several of the boys were recruited into jihadi military training. They were taken to Jakarta and sent to a religious school where they were indoctrinated into Islam. After 11 September, they were required to prove their commitment to "the cause" of Osama bin Laden and were registered to go fight in Afghanistan. As one boy told Baroness Cox, "I was told that

10,000 had already registered and the person behind the mobi-
lization was Amien Ries." Ries was one of the leading
Indonesian politicians at the time.

Stories similar to those Cox heard during her interviews
were reported in London's *Daily Telegraph* a year later. Alex
Spillius filed a story from Ambon headlined "Indonesian
Christians Forced into Islamic Faith: Men and Women were
Circumcised without Anaesthetic". Spillius wrote, "For six
weeks Thomas Rusin was called Hamim, but he is very happy
to be called Thomas again. He was given his new name at gun-
point by a mob in a mosque. He and his family and friends
were told that if they did not convert to Islam they would die.
They had already heard that two Protestant teachers from
another village who had refused had been slaughtered. They
had no choice ... "

In the years since 1999, and following the catastrophic
2002 Bali bombing, South-East Asia has been faced with
spreading, increasing violence. Indonesia teeters on a knife
edge. Will it fall to radical Islamists? President Wahid, serving
as honorary president of IICORR, has written about the need
for moderation in Islam. He concluded a landmark *Wall Street
Journal* article in January 2006 with a challenge to moderate
Muslims:

> *Muslims themselves can and must propagate an under-
> standing of the "right" Islam, and thereby discredit extrem-
> ist ideology. Yet to accomplish this task requires the
> understanding and support of like-minded individuals,
> organizations and governments throughout the world.
> Our goal must be to illuminate the hearts and minds of
> humanity, and offer a compelling alternate vision of
> Islam, one that banishes the fanatical ideology of hatred to
> the darkness from which it emerged.*

"Tell the Whole World The Miracle"

During her visits to Indonesia, Caroline Cox has interviewed scores of people who have suffered at the hands of Islamic militants. She has heard horror stories of attacks and assaults, of fleeing families and narrow escapes. But occasionally she has also heard reports about the kind of divine intervention that can be understood only as a kind of miracle. One such testimony from Christian villagers near Ambon was almost biblical in its drama, and was reportedly witnessed by thousands of believers.

Anis Risameesy, a man aged 38, described events that took place after his village (Waai) had been attacked in July 2000. During the first attack, on 6 July, much of the village was destroyed. Many frightened villagers, expecting further attacks, ran away and hid in the jungle. Anis waited for a while to see what would happen. Before long he saw the attackers regrouping and surrounding the village. Alarmed, he and a local pastor fled and hid in the jungle. Their hearts were pounding as they found a haven in the trees. "I think we should pray," the pastor said quietly. And so they did.

Afterwards the two men walked three to four kilometres from the village until they encountered five more young men, and the pastor decided to stay and look after them. Meanwhile, Anis returned to the village to see what was happening. He witnessed an attack very similar to the first, so he retreated again. He made his way back to the pastor to advise him that it would be impossible to return and that they would have to flee further into the jungle.

Their little group joined the rest of the community that had fled into the hills but soon realized that they were being pursued by some of the attackers. The pastor prayed again. It was 5:30 in the evening. Normally at that time of day it would already have begun to get dark. But that day no darkness fell. Again the pastor prayed.

After he had prayed for the third time, there was

suddenly a very strong light. Anis, the pastor and the young men saw Christ there. In fact, all of the 3,000 people hiding in the area said they, too, saw the light, although only about a dozen actually saw the figure of Christ. However, everyone heard a loud voice proclaiming from the mountain top very clearly: "Be not afraid, I will be with you always."

The voice spoke a second time: "Look, I am coming with my hands open so you can see my scars."

Then the voice spoke directly to the Christian pastor: *"My son, where are you?"*

The pastor knelt and replied, *"I am your son ... "*

He said later that, despite the supernatural aspects of the vision, he still somehow felt as if he were talking to a close friend. While he was still kneeling, the figure of Christ came close and touched him. The Lord spoke once again: "Do not be afraid. I will be with you always. Stand up and walk."

Then, according to those who experienced this event, thick clouds descended, cutting off the approach of the jihad warriors. The refugees went on their way, trying to reach Passo, their destination.

Ordinarily the walk to Passo through the jungle would have taken four days and nights; on this occasion the people accomplished the journey in just two days. They later reported that on that first night it never got dark; daylight continued throughout the night. Anis explained, "It was as if a huge flashlight was covering us as we made our way. We felt amazed and very blessed. We knew that God wanted us to be witnesses for Him so we decided to tell the whole world about the miracle we had experienced."

To Lady Cox, who was listening with rapt attention, Anis said, "I think this interview itself is a miracle. There's no way I could go around the world to tell what happened. But God sent you here, and now we can share the story of our miracle through you!"

Increasing Islamization, Increasing Danger to Christians

Violence against Christians in Indonesia continues. A bombing in the predominantly Christian village of Tentena in May 2005 left 22 dead and at least 74 injured. Another bomb exploded on New Year's Eve 2005, at a predominantly Christian-area market in Palu, Central Sulawesi, killing eight people and injuring 56.

Months later, the Associated Press reported the beheadings of the three Christian teenagers on 29 October 2005. Six men attacked four girls – Theresia Morangke, fifteen, Alfita Poliwo, 17, Yarni Sambue, fifteen, and Noviana Malewa, fifteen – early in the morning as they walked to a Christian school in Poso district. The first three girls were beheaded; Noviana Malewa received serious injuries to her face and neck but survived the attack.

The girls' heads were wrapped in black plastic bags. One was found on the steps of a Kasiguncu village church. The other two were left at a nearby police station. One of the bags contained a note, some of which read, "We will murder 100 more Christian teenagers and their heads will be presented as presents."

In September, 2006, a pastor and his pregnant wife, living in Aceh province, Indonesia, fled their home after a Muslim mob set fire to their church building. Several weeks earlier, Pastor Luther Saragih had sent letters to Christians in several surrounding villages inviting them to a revival service. Local Muslims intercepted the letter, reworded it and then publicized their version, claiming that it was an invitation to Muslims, not Christians, sent with the intention of proselytizing them.

Over 500 Christians arrived for the service. A huge crowd of infuriated Muslims also showed up and the service was cut short by police intervention. Later that night the mob poured petrol round the building and set fire to it; they also attempted to burn a second building used as a church kinder-garten. The pastor and his wife fled and were hidden and looked after by Christians in another area.

Weeks later, *Compass Direct News Service* reported that two more schoolgirls – Siti Nuraini and her friend Ivon Maganti, both 17 – had been shot in the face on 8 November. Nuraini died from her wounds but Maganti survived the attack

Also in 2006, three Indonesian Christian men – Fabianus Tibo, Dominggus da Silva and Marinus Riwu – were condemned to death for their alleged roles in inter-religious violence that had taken place in central Sulawesi in 2000. It was widely believed that crowds of Muslim hardliners, who gathered at the court during the men's hearings, had intimi-dated the judges, barristers and witnesses. After the death sen-tence was passed, there were widespread calls for a retrial. The executions took place despite an appeal by Pope Benedict XVI and a host of religious and political leaders across the world to spare the men.

In her letter to the Indonesian Ambassador to Great Britain, Baroness Cox wrote, in part, "May I and my colleagues add our voices to the voices of many others who are pleading for a stay of execution ... we are deeply disturbed ... I hope you will understand that this is not only a matter of great anxiety for the plight of these three convicted men and their families, but also a matter of grave international concern for human rights, justice and due process."

The three men were executed on 22 September 2006. Christian groups and human rights organizations around the world have since voiced their concern over fears that the Indonesian government was using the men as scapegoats in order to placate Islamic radicals.

Al Jazeera's English-language website reported on 12 January 2007 that "Central Sulawesi has been tense since the execution of the three Christian fighters over their role in the sectarian clashes between Muslim and Christian mobs that gripped the region from 1998 to 2001. In October, an armed group clashed with police and set fire to a Christian church in Poso, while a priest was shot in Palu, sparking fears of a resurgence in sectarian violence. Three years of clashes in Central Sulawesi killed more than 2,000 people before a peace accord took effect in late 2001." [http://english.aljazeera.net/NR/exeres/590535A1-6E2B-4013-8552-7CBAC0779F1.htm]

In fact, many observers are alarmed at the Indonesian government's perceived capitulation to radical Islamists. In June 2006 journalist Ridwan Max Sijabat wrote in the *Jakarta Post*: "Indonesia will turn into an Islamic state if the government does nothing to counter the violence committed by hardline religious groups or the repressive Shari'a-inspired bylaws passed by local governments... Dozens of regions across the country have enacted Shari'a-style bylaws... Muslim hardliners, meanwhile, have launched a series of violent attacks..."

As Sijabat reported, the outlook for Indonesia's survival as a thriving democracy embracing religious freedom is precarious. Still, as in all the world's darkest corners, the light of faith shines brightly.

Though the Cause of Evil Prosper...

One example of a person of radiant faith is described by Caroline Cox in her book *Cox's Book of Modern Saints and Martyrs*: Indonesian pastor Rinaldy Damanik. Caroline went to visit him in a prison cell in Palu, Central Sulawesi. She wrote, "I had gone to this beautiful but conflict-scarred island to demonstrate international interest in Reverend Damanik's trial, scheduled for the next morning."

The previous year, Damanik and others had been evacuating Christians from a village that had been attacked by jihadists when their vehicles were stopped by a mob of Muslims. Soon the police arrived, but they appeared to be complicit in the mob scene. They searched Damanik's car and soon declared that they had found illegal weapons in his possession.

There was ample evidence that Damanik had been framed by the authorities. Even his accusers could not agree on the number of weapons they had supposedly discovered in his vehicle. Nevertheless, he was arrested and sent to prison.

When Caroline Cox met Rev. Damanik, whom she described as "a man with a joyful, warm smile, who radiated happiness and love", he explained to her that he had been offered freedom if he would plead guilty. But, he argued, he could not plead guilty because he was not guilty. Truth was more important to him than freedom. The next morning Cox sat in the courtroom. She describes the scene:

Just in front of me stood Rinaldy Damanik, alone, defenceless – except for the defence of the truth. Representing himself, he addressed the three judges seated on the platform above him:

"Your Honours, my defence is not for judges but for the state of Indonesia. What I am doing in opposing mis-representation with the truth is not in order to justify myself but for the peace of Poso and its surrounding areas. We have responsibility not only for the present time, but for our children, our grandchildren and future genera-tions… we have responsibility not only for Christians but for all victims.

"I have been offered my freedom if I will plead guilty. But that I cannot do because I am not guilty. I can-not accept freedom on the basis of a lie. We cannot build the future for our children, for our grandchildren, for Indonesia on the basis of a lie. Even if I must spend many years in prison, even if I must go to the scaffold, I would prefer to go to the scaffold for the truth than to accept free-dom for a lie…"

Despite testimony that was obviously contrived and laden with falsehood, and despite glaring irregularities in the proceedings, Damanik was sentenced to three years in prison.

Whenever she speaks of Rinaldy Damanik, Caroline Cox recalls sitting in that courtroom, a few feet away from him, hearing him choose the possibility of execution on a scaffold rather than freedom at the cost of agreeing to a tell a lie – and how the verse of a great hymn went through her mind again and again:

> *Though the cause of evil prosper,*
> *Yet 'tis Truth alone is strong:*
> *Though her portion be the scaffold,*
> *And upon the throne be Wrong –*
> *Yet that scaffold sways the future,*
> *And behind the dim unknown,*
> *Standeth God within the shadow,*
> *Keeping watch above his own.*
>
> (James Russell Lowell 1819–1891)

The next time Caroline saw Rev. Damanik was in November 2005 in England at the House of Lords. He had been released several months early, which he attributed to international prayer and pressure on the Indonesian authorities. He greeted her with the same radiant smile she remembered from their first encounter in his prison cell. He said, "Lady Cox, when you came to that prison, it was like seeing an angel; it was like a miracle – that someone from the West, a politician, cared enough to come to my trial…"

EAST TIMOR

CHAPTER SIX

East Timor – A Hungry Little Land

Baroness Cox's efforts have not stopped at Indonesia's borders. On the tip of the Indonesian archipelago lies East Timor (also known as Timor-Leste), with a population of almost a million people. It is the world's newest nation and Asia's poorest. Like Indonesia, it was occupied by the Japanese from 1942 to 1945, when Portugal resumed its colonial rule. East Timor declared independence on 28 November 1975. Indonesia invaded nine days later and two decades of fighting followed, in which an estimated 100,000 to 250,000 people were killed.

On 30 August 1999, in a referendum organized by the United Nations, an overwhelming majority voted for independence. An Indonesian-backed militia retaliated with a massive scorched-earth campaign. Approximately 1,400 Timorese were killed, and 300,000 people were driven into West Timor as refugees. A large part of the country's infrastructure was ruined, including homes and schools; the water supply together with irrigation systems and most of the electrical grid were destroyed. Eventually, after three years of UN-administered transition, on 20 May 2002 East Timor became an independent state.

In 2006, however, after four years of relative stability and peace, violence broke out again, particularly in the capital, Dili. The tragedy is that this time the conflict took place between different East Timorese factions, rather than between the Timorese and foreign occupiers. The factors that contributed to the turmoil included political conflict at the very heart of government, widespread unemployment, poverty, factionalism and the breakdown of law and order.

The violence drove an estimated 25,000 people in Dili, the capital city, from their homes. It brought about the burning of countless houses, and the killing of perhaps as many as 300 people. The UN returned to restore order and provide assistance to the East Timorese government, particularly in the form of police and peacekeepers. But by then those thousands of people who had fled their homes were living in camps. Meanwhile, some of Dili's neighbourhoods were reduced to wastelands of bombed, burnt-out buildings.

Not surprisingly, East Timor also faces significant challenges in the area of health care, particularly regarding malnutrition, death in childbirth and infant mortality. UNICEF reported in 2005: "In Timor-Leste, malnutrition is a common and serious problem.... 42.6% are underweight and 46.7% have suffered stunting and wasting."

Representing HART (the Humanitarian Aid Relief Trust), Caroline Cox visited East Timor in November 2006 to obtain up-to-date information on the challenges there. She had visited the Timorese twice previously, and under her leadership HART had developed a partnership with Hiam Health Clinic's Malnutrition Rehabilitation Centre.

Hiam Health is a local NGO established to give support to in- and outpatients at Dili National Hospital (DNH) and sub-district clinics. It focuses on people in extreme poverty who have no means of support while they are away from their villages and families. Hiam Health staff now provide several services, including the following-up of infants and children with malnutrition, compulsory daily workshops on health and nutrition for parents and caregivers, and palliative and pastoral care for patients in hospitals and after discharge.

In late 2006, Caroline Cox wrote:

In East Timor, HART has been supporting a primary health care clinic. When we went to the clinic on our last visit, we were very impressed by the professionalism of the staff and the effectiveness of their programmes. We were especially impressed by the rural outreach projects to remote areas where people are still suffering from serious shortages of provision of health care and food.

We had thought the situation might be improving to such an extent that this would no longer be a priority area for HART. However, the recent flare-up of large-scale violence, with the associated evacuation of many aid personnel, has led us to plan to revisit East Timor at a later date to assess the situation and the need for further assistance.

Although the people of East Timor have suffered so greatly, they are still fiercely independent and resilient. They are predominantly Christian and count among their number an amazing Catholic sister who maintains a small community in the mountainous jungle high above Dili. Sister Maria Lourdes exhibits resilience and faith in abundance. She is also associated with a situation that she recalls as nothing short of miraculous. She describes what happened when the war for independence was at its height:

When fighting in East Timor was at its worst, 15,000 people left the city and found refuge in the jungle around my house. We did not have enough food for even fifteen people, let alone, 15,000. But each day I got up, I prayed, and then I started cooking rice. And the barrel of rice never ran out for three weeks. On the day when the international peacekeepers arrived and it was safe for the people to return to Dili, the rice container resumed its normal behaviour and the supply ran out. God worked a miracle!

East Timor is still inherently vulnerable. It is hard to maintain democracy for people with empty stomachs. Meanwhile, for years there have been calls from radical Muslims to reclaim this island for Islam. In November 2001, in a speech broadcast on the *Al-Jazeera* satellite television network, Osama bin Laden included East Timor in a long tirade against the West, listed among global targets for his radical jihadi movement. He said,

"The crusader Australian forces were on Indonesian shores, and in fact they landed to separate East Timor, which is part of the Islamic world. Therefore, we should view events not as separate links, but as links in a long series of conspiracies, a war of annihilation in the true sense of the word."

Much is at stake, not only for the people of East Timor who have suffered so greatly, but also for the wider region. Still, questions remain: will this fragile new democracy survive? Can its citizens preserve the freedom for which they have paid so high a price?

NIGERIA

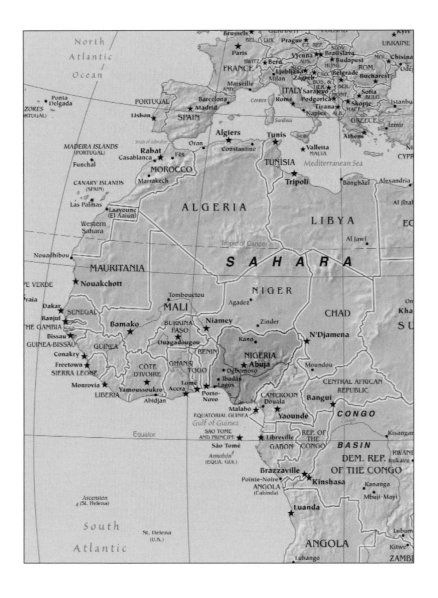

CHAPTER SEVEN

Nigeria – "Will You Tell the World?"

Nigerian Bishop Ben's beautiful smile is a kind of miracle. It's hard to imagine that a man with such a radiant, joyful countenance could have looked upon as much suffering as he has. And yet, like so many of Nigeria's beleaguered Christians, the Rt Rev. Dr Benjamin Argak Kwashi somehow manages to find happiness and serenity in the midst of devastating circumstances. Like Bishop Ben, Nigeria's believers are an inspiration in the midst of their distress, which is both intense and intensifying.

Bishop Ben Kwashi was born in 1955, studied at the Theological College of Northern Nigeria and was ordained in 1982. He has served in Christian ministry in both rural and urban areas, working tirelessly and faithfully. In 1987 his church and home were burned to the ground in Christian–Muslim riots. In 1992 he was consecrated and enthroned as Bishop of Jos, and under his leadership several schools, a Christian Institute and health care programmes have been established, including special care for a very large number of HIV/AIDS patients – both Muslim and Christian. Bishop Ben is married to Gloria Ladi Kwashi, and they have six children.

Caroline expresses special admiration and affection for Gloria. "She is always ready to help when a village is attacked by Islamist militants, filling a bus with clothes, cooking pots – whatever is needed – and driving into the troubled areas. My nickname for her is 'Gloria in Excelsis'."

Gloria's concern for those attacked by terrorists came close to home in February 2006, when jihadis broke into the Kwashis' own house. They weren't just interested in robbery or vandalism – their intention was to murder Bishop Ben. He was not at home, so they attacked his family instead. They savagely beat two of his sons, one so fiercely that he lost consciousness. But they saved their worst violence for Gloria. They sexually assaulted her. They beat her. They subjected her to such severe torture that she lost her eyesight. Before leaving, the assailants also attacked members of the Bishop's staff and stole significant amounts of money belonging to the diocese.

When Bishop Ben was notified of the cruelty meted out to his family – an attack that was intended for him – he rushed back to Jos. Ben's immediate message to friends abroad was a request to the authorities to provide adequate security for his community. The next day, his subsequent messages were profoundly inspiring examples of forgiveness, resilience, courage and even humour. He wrote:

> We have been surrounded by love, support and prayers. Last night, I had a good laugh at myself when I just sat down and thought about my life… My life and that of my family seems to be in constant danger and inviting the prayers of the church of God around the world. Maybe I should get into more trouble… !!! The testimony of the recent happenings is the miraculous healing that the prayer of the church has brought upon Gloria, myself, the children and the entire diocese. Her recovery is remarkable… The surgery was a huge success. She is healing steadily and she was able to sit down to take Holy Communion last night. Her speech is restored even though it is a bit slow and weak. We shared jokes yesterday and she had a great time of laughter… We are praying that our sufferings, and specifically that the humiliation, blood, tears and pains of Gloria, may bring tremendous glory to God…

Baroness Cox's first visit to Nigeria took place in 1998, shortly after an Anglican conference at Lambeth Palace, the Archbishop of Canterbury's headquarters, from which many African clergy and bishops returned to their homes feeling demoralized and alienated. In Jos during her first conversation with Bishop Ben, Lady Cox asked him if he and his brother bishops felt that the Anglican Church had any real feeling for the persecuted church. Temporarily, he lost his happy smile. "No. I and my brother bishops feel very sad and alone," he admitted. "Indeed, we felt so alone that we turned to God and said our prayers – which, perhaps, being bishops, we should have done already. And now you have come. You are an answer to our prayers. Will you tell the world what is happening here in Nigeria?"

Subsequently, Baroness Cox did just that. Through her organization, HART, money was sent to people suffering from the conflicts in Jos and elsewhere in Plateau State. She says, "We continue to be amazed to see relatively small sums of money used in ways which exceed any expectations. For example, one English country church gave a generous donation of 2,000 pounds. Moved by this generosity. I decided to dedicate the entire amount to one place, so I asked the vicar to select one of the areas where we are working. Nigeria was chosen. A few months later, our HART team visited Jos and asked to see how the church's donation had been used. The 2,000 pounds had been used to rebuild four churches and three schools."

Late one evening Caroline Cox visited the remote village where that church's money had been put to use in rebuilding a church that had been destroyed in the jihad. She received a rapturous welcome. Villagers appeared, seemingly out of nowhere, their smiles lighting up the darkness. "We have lost everything in this conflict," one of them told her, "and we were in despair. We had no idea how we were ever going to rebuild anything, including our precious church. Then we suddenly heard that you were coming. We learned that people far away loved us and cared enough to help us rebuild our community.

We are so grateful! And now we have a building, new people are coming to join us and our church family is growing."

Caroline returned to Britain on Friday evening. On Saturday, she downloaded her photos onto PowerPoint; on Sunday morning she was back in the same pulpit, showing the pictures and saying a heartfelt "Thank you" to the congregation for the difference they had made for these people so far away. She pointed out that the Nigerians they'd reached out to had thought they were forgotten, but instead had learned that there are people who do love and care for them. The generous congregation was deeply moved – and promptly gave another £4,000 – which Caroline quickly sent to Bishop Ben.

The Battle Over Shari'a Law

Nigeria is Africa's most populous nation, nearly equally divided between Muslims and Christian, with most Muslims located in the country's northern states. Those states have been ravaged by conflict, frequently associated with religious issues. Brutality and bloodshed have increased dramatically during the past 20 years, due to the imposition and implementation of Shari'a (Islamic) law. Christians, along with some moderate Muslims and others, have resisted this radical Islamist agenda with great determination, and their resistance has often led to violence. It is estimated that as many as 60,000 women, men and children have perished – many of them Christians. There has also been a massive destruction of property.

To date, twelve Nigerian states either have implemented Shari'a law or are in the process of doing so. Their radical leaders will accept no alternative to Islam's radical legal system. Their reasons are explained succinctly by author and historian Mervyn Hiskett, who writes in *The Sword of Truth*:

> Islam has been emphatic that any aspect of culture that is inconsistent with the Sacred Law has no legitimacy and should not be considered binding on society… Indeed,

Islam does not accept that people should have customs or traditions other than religious ones; for if Allah's way is a comprehensive way of life, what room is there for custom and tradition?

The fact that twelve states have already adopted Shari'a law is greeted with foreboding by the Christian community. Once Shari'a has been extended to 19 of Nigeria's 36 states, there will be a majority and it could be possible to change the Constitution so that Nigeria itself will become an Islamic nation. The impact of this on the non-Muslim population would be catastrophic.

Wherever Shari'a rules, Christians (and Jews – both are identified in Islam as "People of the Book") are assigned *dhimmi* status. According to Islamic tradition, a *dhimmi* is a second- or third-class citizen who implicitly acknowledges the supremacy of Muslim rule, pays a special tax (*jizya*), and has fewer legal rights than Muslims. During a meeting with Lady Cox, leaders of a Shari'a court in Kano acknowledged that it is perfectly acceptable Islamic practice to deceive or defraud Christians in any way deemed necessary to further the cause of Islam. Therefore, under the Shari'a system, any reassurances or promises given to "people of the book" can always be broken with moral impunity.

Muslims also suffer under Shari'a law. In February 2004 Paul Marshall wrote in *National Review Online*:

As with other countries where extremist Islam is growing, the Saudis are active in Nigeria. In mid-January, they offered to finance the employment of Islamic religious teachers and preachers in Kebbi, another of the northern Nigerian states that have adopted Shari'a law. The Saudi Religious and Cultural Attachheik Abdul-Aziz, said that his government had been monitoring the implementation of Shari'a there and noted the results "... with delight. The fundamental human rights of the non-Muslim have not been infringed"... but he was notably silent about the

2

fundamental human rights of Muslims. Apart from the five women and two men who have been sentenced to death by stoning for adultery, Muslims have had their hands amputated as a penalty for theft or their eyes removed as a penalty for injury. And there are many Muslims amongst the over 10,000 dead in Shari'a-induced violence.

Shari'a has been associated with escalating discrimination affecting Muslims as well as non-Muslims. Special religious police (*Hisba*) are trained to enforce Shari'a law. They have no legal status under Nigerian law, yet although they are not properly constituted police: they are permitted by state governments to arrest, jail and intimidate; and they are seen as agents of coercion, intimidation and harassment by many Muslims as well as others. But despite the lack of agreement among Muslims regarding the Shari'a system, its authorities defend it fiercely. During one of her visits to Nigeria, Baroness Cox met Shari'a court officials in Kano. She describes the event:

We were received by the acting Chief Kadir of the Shari'a Court in Kano, the Chief Registrar Mr Ismail Ahad. Mr Ismail claimed that the implementation of Shari'a law was nothing new in Kano. It had been implemented in pre-colonial days – except, he explained, for those parts of the criminal aspects of the law that called for amputations and other extreme physical punishments. These had not been allowed previously. Now, however, the full Shari'a was being implemented ... the Chief Registrar repeated more than once that Shari'a operates only for Muslims, and that he could never envisage the possibility of full Shari'a in Nigeria. But he did admit that "Shari'a is above all and over all and is in fact above the Constitution. Within five years we will amend the constitution for Shari'a law".

Nigerian Jihad

Protected by Shari'a law, jihadists sometimes attack Christians without legal repercussions. In 2003, Caroline Cox visited Kassa, a village outside Jos. For years, Muslims and Christians had lived peacefully together there. But, little by little, Muslims who lived in the village began to sell their houses to their Christian neighbours, and by October 2002 they had nearly all relocated elsewhere. Just after midnight on 14 October, armed tribesmen attacked the village assisted by mercenaries, possibly from Chad and Niger. According to the villagers, the attack was carefully planned and systematic. The armed men invaded from three different directions. The houses that had been sold to Christians by Muslims were specifically targeted for burning. Those who lived in them had virtually no warning of the attack.

Most of the villagers were sound asleep when they suddenly heard gunshots and men shouting "Allah-u-Akbar!" The jihadis converged on the village, shooting randomly. As the terrified victims fled into the surrounding bushes, their assailants doused their houses with petrol, set light to them and burned them to the ground. Five villagers were killed in the attack, including one old man who was murdered in his house. Another man died trying to stop the attackers from destroying his shop, along with a woman and a child. When the attack began, a few of villagers drove their cars to the local police station, assuming the vehicles would be safe under police protection. But the police also fled once the attack was under way. The jihadis not only outnumbered them but were also far better armed. Meanwhile, all the cars that were in the police compound were torched and destroyed.

A 40-year-old woman, Chundung Danielle, was sleeping in her hut with her husband and children when the sound of gunshots awakened them all. Her husband panicked and fled the house, leaving Danielle alone with their children. She was nine months pregnant at the time. A gang of terrorists burst into the house and demanded that she tell them where her husband was.

"He's not here … he ran away," she cried.

In response, the attackers started beating her and the children, brandishing knives. One cautioned the others, "We aren't supposed to attack women and children!"

At his word, most of them retreated. But two of the thugs were unmoved – they slashed at the mother and children with their knives. Then, for good measure, one of them shot Danielle in the stomach. They left her bleeding and in a grave condition. Not until the next morning was she rushed to hospital, where she underwent emergency surgery. Her baby was delivered alive, but has since died.

More recently, on 18 April 2006, a serious outbreak of violence erupted in Namu after a Christian boy was killed. Caroline Cox also visited that village and learned that the trouble had begun over the allocation of land. While the quarrelling continued, the local emir quietly gathered a group of Muslim mercenaries, keeping them out of sight. Then the Christian boy was murdered. Fighting immediately broke out, and it suddenly erupted into large-scale violence when the Muslim mercenaries joined the fray.

On this occasion, however, the main casualties were the mercenaries themselves. Their commander was killed and his soldiers apparently lost their way and could not escape. At least 60 people lost their lives (some estimate that the number could have been as high as 200), and there were many more casualties. Numerous properties were burned, the majority of them belonging to Christians. Only two Muslim properties were destroyed in a neighbourhood that remained substantially intact. There is still widespread tension in Namu, and fear of further violence. Small-scale but serious incidents continue to occur with disturbing frequency.

In yet another confrontation on 24 June 2006, armed robbers attacked a home on the campus of Jos State University. Canon Emmanuel Ajulo was dining at home with his family when armed robbers broke into the house, robbed and looted the premises, and then fled. Ajulo claims that the police took no effective action.

The Ajulo incident is not an aberration. Nigerian Christian communities in the northern states continue to report a long-standing failure of the police to take effective action to prevent or respond to attacks. A prime example comes from Bishop Ben Kwashi himself. Although the police were telephoned immediately when his wife and family were so savagely assaulted, three hours passed before any officers arrived on the scene. Local leaders argue that both state and federal governments are appeasing the militants, and their refusal to take appropriate measures is causing mounting frustration in the Christian communities. They also claim that, on occasions when Christians do defend themselves, police arrest the Christians and blame them for being the aggressors.

Devastation in Kano State

Caroline Cox heard about the danger faced by Christians in Kano State during a visit to the Anglican Bishop of Kano, the Rt Rev. Zakka Lalle Nyam. Along with other Christian leaders, Bishop Nyam revealed story after story of Christians who had been killed and churches that had been destroyed. "They assured me," she said later, "that a Muslim who kills a Christian pastor receives a 'reward' of a sum equivalent to a month's average wage."

Later, in 2004, Bishop Nyam distributed a report about riots that had taken place in Kano that summer. He wrote, "It is estimated that well over 3,000 people were killed and property worth over 500 million nyra destroyed… Most, if not all, church buildings at Panshakara, Shagari quarters, Zango, Brigade, Namibia, Sheka and Challawa and some in Badawa were all burnt down." Bishop Nyam's report continued:

> *Some of the stories that happened are too inhuman to tell. [They are so appalling that readers may find them hard to*

believe, and we quote only those we learned from respected and reputable sources. And although they may seem exaggerated beyond belief to those unfamiliar with such situations, they are, tragically, not untypical.] For example, at Sharada, a seven-day old baby belonging to a Tyoruba family was said to have been fried alive in boiling oil on the day of its christening. The parents had invited guests to the naming ceremony of the poor child and when this was taking place the militants arrived and attacked. Everyone took to his or her heels, leaving the baby (who was in the house calmly sleeping) to the mercy of the jihadists. Without qualms ... the child was picked up and thrown into the boiling oil; as it continued to whine until it died the jihadists danced round the pot chanting and shrieking in an obscene way and brandishing their weapons ... [This story was told by a participant who begged to remain anonymous.]

These brutalities took place against a backdrop of systematic oppression of Christians. Compared with such violence, incidents of discrimination can seem innocuous, but they bear witness to the disdain with which Christians are treated in Kano State. For example, the first Anglican church built in Kano, at Fagge, was overcrowded, and the then Primate of the Anglican Communion, Archbishop Robert Runcie, laid the foundation stone of a new church on 29 April 1982. The building was partially erected, but then the government forbade further development. The reason given – and this explanation was given only verbally – was that Muslims worshipping in an adjacent mosque, which had been built long after the church was founded, would be offended by the sight of a church while praying. It would be impossible to build a wall sufficiently high to shield them from the sight of the church as they lifted their eyes towards heaven in prayer. To this day, the church remains only partially built. A committee of inquiry has been established, but no report has yet been published.

As the Bishop of Kano said, "They do not make it easy for us to live with them."

Another more distressing issue, especially in areas under the jurisdiction of Shari'a courts, concerns the problems facing Muslims who convert to Christianity. Having committed apostasy, as defined in Islamic law, their lives are at risk – at the hands of their own families and communities; they call it "honour killing". If they run away and seek sanctuary elsewhere, they are still in danger of being hunted down, typically by young zealots who kill them, often by decapitation.

Those who are not killed are taken away with the intention of reconverting them to Islam. Christian churches spend a great amount of time and resources providing such persons with protection and the opportunity to develop a new life. It is important to remember that these converts have exercised a fundamental freedom – to change their religious beliefs – in accordance with the Universal Declaration of Human Rights, to which Nigeria is a signatory.

Despite all these challenges, Bishop Nyam emphasized the resilience of the Nigerian Christian church and the resolve of individual believers. Christian churches continue to grow in size and number. "If they kill 200 Christian people and destroy a church," he says with a smile, "within a few years, there will be 200 more Christians – for the blood of the martyrs is the seed of the church."

In conversations with Caroline Cox, Christian leaders in Kano likened their experiences under the Islamic regime to that of a people in captivity. They said Christians are oppressed, discriminated against and humiliated because of their faith. An atmosphere of intimidation prevails since a massive outbreak of violence in 2004. Bishop Foster Ekeleme, Methodist Bishop of Kano and the State Chairman of CAN, described how Christians were attacked in Kano that May:

> *Muslim leaders in Kano assembled Muslims at the central mosque in this city on 11 May 2004. This was at about 2am. They incited them against Christians. Muslims in*

> *government were also in the mosque to incite their fellow*
> *Muslims against us. It was from the mosque at about 5:30*
> *am that these Muslims trooped onto the streets and began*
> *attacking Christians, killing Christians they came across,*
> *and burning churches and homes of Christians.*

According to Bishop Ekeleme, 1,750 Christians were killed, including ten pastors; 30 churches were burned, and 30,000 Christians were displaced. Such violence and sustained discrimination have caused many humanitarian problems, including the devastation of schools and health care facilities and, of course, an increase in widows and orphans.

Life and Death in Bauchi State

Bauchi State is bordered by, among other states, Kano, Plateau and Kaduna. And, like its neighbours, Bauchi suffers from Islamic militancy. In 1995, Gungu Village in Bauchi State was attacked by a large force of Muslims. In the midst of their assault, they told a group of terrified Christians that if the women took refuge in the church they would be safe. Twenty-two women fled into the church. But instead of finding a haven, they were slaughtered with bullets and knives. Twenty-eight other villagers, men, women and children, were massacred outside the church.

The village was the target of a second attack in 2002. On this occasion the villagers fled, so there were no casualties. But the attackers completely destroyed both the Protestant and the Catholic churches.

After the village was attacked for the third time, Caroline Cox met Rev. Canon Chuk and other Christian leaders, and received an account of the most recent outbreak of violence, which erupted in February 2006. Twenty-seven people are known to have died during this massacre. As of June 2006 their bodies were still being held in the mortuary. Repeated requests for their release for proper burial had not yet been met. The total number of dead may never be known, as many people who fled have not yet dared to return. It is not clear whether some of the missing have been killed.

"The latest violence was triggered by an incident in Command Secondary School," Caroline Cox explains, "where a girl student insisted in reading the Koran so loudly during an English lesson that it was impossible for the teacher to continue to teach. The student continued reading aloud, despite requests from the teacher to desist. The teacher then did what any teacher would do to silence the distraction: he took the Koran away from the student. A group of young men were outside, apparently awaiting this turn of events. In response to the young woman's cries that the teacher had committed blasphemy, they promptly ran into the town, shouting out that the Koran had been defiled. Immediately violence erupted, with resulting killings and destruction of buildings. As one of the Christian leaders said, 'We must live with one eye open all the time. In the morning we are friends, but in the evening they become our enemies.'"

Christians: Unwarned and Unprepared

In Kaduna, Nigeria, during an outbreak of serious violence in 2000, 400 churches were destroyed.

In another uprising, in November 2002, 120 churches were destroyed and 210 Christians were killed including four clergymen: a Catholic priest, a Baptist pastor, a Pentecostal pastor and a Methodist minister. If there is a subsequent flare-up of violence, more churches will be destroyed, effectively leaving no registered churches standing in Kaduna city or its outskirts. In fact, there are virtually no churches left in the central areas of the cities of Kaduna, Kano and Bauchi.

As Caroline Cox travelled around in the northern states, listening to bishops and clergy describing events that had taken place during the Nigerian riots and violence, it was apparent to her that the Christians, unlike their Muslim neighbours, had no forewarning of the impending attacks. For example, a teacher would go to school as usual, and find his Muslim colleagues and students absent; or an employer would go to work and find his Muslim workers had not turned up. Often the Christians were unprepared for the ensuing violence, in a state of panic about what was happening to their families, and without a clear policy on how to protect themselves, their homes, their businesses or their places of worship. By contrast, the Muslim communities had strategic plans, had time to put them in place, and were able to maintain a level of secrecy.

Some Christian communities have been agonizing over the dilemma of how to respond to riots and attacks on their communities. Initially they adopted the theological position of "turning the other cheek", generally desisting from retaliation. However, as attacks continued, they began to defend themselves and also to counter-attack. For instance, the Center for Religious Freedom at Hudson Institute reports:

> On 18 February 2006, during "Danish Cartoon Riots," about 50 Christians and 57 churches and 250 Christian businesses were destroyed by rioting Muslims in the north-easterly city of Maiduguri in Borno State. Some witnesses report seeing the Governor of Borno giving out money to the mob. In response to the killings, Igbo youths in southern Nigeria carried out retaliatory attacks on Muslims.

With regard to Muslim–Christian violence, Caroline Cox and her colleagues have tried to obtain figures relating to Muslim casualties and the extent of destruction of property, but have so far been unsuccessful. However, anecdotal impressions have indicated that there is obvious asymmetry both in the initiation of violence and in the extent of the ensuing suffering. More attacks seem to be instigated by Muslims (now often with external well-armed mercenary reinforcements) and more loss of life and property suffered by Christians than by Muslim communities. Lady Cox comments:

This brings us back to where we began: the issues confronting Nigeria today are not new. They have deep historical roots and they present dilemmas which need urgent consideration. They include:

- *the significance for Christians of Shari'a law in states where it has already been implemented;*
- *the implications of the possibility of a change in the Constitution;*
- *the escalation of violence with the involvement of foreign jihadi mercenaries;*
- *the appropriate responses to the present situation by the Christian and Muslim communities.*

Shari'a law in Nigeria provides ample reason for concern – not only for Christians but for all who come under the authority of Shari'a courts. The US State Department's 2006 Report on Religious Freedom cites several examples of Shari'a court decisions:

In September 2004 in Bauchi State, Daso Adamu, a nursing mother, was sentenced to death by stoning when she initially admitted to having sex with her first husband after her second husband absconded. The man was freed for lack of evidence. In October 2004 she was released on bail on the grounds that she was breastfeeding. In December 2004 a Shari'a appeals court vacated the conviction and sentence, ruling that her pregnancy was insufficient evidence to convict her.

In October 2004 in Bauchi State, Hajara Ibrahim was sentenced to death by stoning for adultery after becoming pregnant outside of wedlock. According to the Shari'a court that convicted her, she confessed to having sex with a man who had promised to marry her. The man denied meeting her and was released for lack of evidence. The defendant appealed the sentence, stating that she should have been charged with the lesser crime of fornication, rather than adultery. In November 2005 a Shari'a appeals court overturned the conviction and sentence, ruling that she had never consummated an arranged marriage and therefore should never have been charged with adultery. It appeared that the prosecution in the case had not pursued the fornication charge subsequent to the court's ruling.

The Nigeria Legal Aid Council agreed to appeal thirty Shari'a convictions and death sentences in Bauchi State. In one case from September 2004, an eighteen-year-old man, Saleh Dabo, alleged that police told him he could plead guilty to rape and he would be released; instead, a court sentenced him to death by stoning for adultery, even though he was not married. At the end of the period covered by this report, the appeal had not been heard, and the sentence had not been carried out.

A Nigeria-style Miracle

Northern Nigeria is a deeply divided and troubled land where countless Christians have paid for their faith with their lives. Travelling in such regions can be a risky business. There are multiple dangers, not only involving terrorism but also disease, snake and insect bites, robbery, kidnapping and unreliable forms of transport. But, as is often the case, where things seem darkest, light shines through. When describing the state of affairs in Nigeria, with a twinkle in her eyes, Cox cannot resist sharing another of those miracles she loves to report:

We were driving from Kaduna to Abuja – about 200 miles through empty bush. We had to catch a plane that night, and we had the cheapest airline tickets possible – non-transferable, non-refundable, non-returnable, almost non-usable. If you miss your flight, these were the kind of tickets no other airline wants to know about.

There was a debate on Africa in the House of Lords the next day and I wanted to speak on Nigeria. We had to get the flight! However, our Nigerian hosts had cut the timing very fine so we were driving extremely fast, anxiously clock-watching.

Suddenly a car going the other way urgently flashed us down. He disappeared in the dust and we swerved to a halt by the roadside to see why he had stopped us. I am no mechanic but my heart sank. Oil was pouring from one of the rear wheels. So there we were, stuck in empty bush, with no village, let alone a garage, anywhere on the horizon.

We were a pretty useless group, so we just said our prayers and waited. Then, all at once, from between the bushes, there appeared two very competent young men, who immediately opened the boot, took out the tool kit and removed the wheel.

Wonderful! we thought. But our comfort didn't last long. As the wheel came off, the wheel bearings fell onto the road. Again, I'm no mechanic, but I know you need wheel bearings to drive a car. So we prayed again.

Minutes later, out of that empty bush there came a lad aged about 12, carrying a black plastic bag. And out of that bag came a brand new set of wheel bearings which fitted our Honda car. The team of competent mechanics put them in and replaced the wheel. They then asked us to drive for a few yards to check the balance. Oil gushed from other rear wheel. We sank back into despair. But then off came that wheel, back came the boy with the black plastic bag and out came a second set of wheel bearings for a Honda.

The car was on the road in 20 minutes. Can you imagine such prompt service anywhere in London, New York or anywhere in our "civilized Western world"?

Baroness Cox arrived at the airport in time to catch her flight, returned safely to London and, as hoped, summarized for the House of Lords what she had learned on her latest journey to Nigeria, which had concluded just hours before. She addressed her peers at 9:36 pm on 2 December 2003, as recorded in that day's *Hansard*:

> *... I briefly turn to Nigeria, having returned yesterday from a visit which was related to several serious issues that threaten Nigeria's development of civil society and a stable democracy. I refer to the conflicts that are occurring with disturbing frequency in the northern states associated with the imposition of Shari'a law, which is now in force in 12 states. In January, I visited Jos, Kaduna, Kano and Bauchi states, which have all been subjected to violence in which hundreds of people have been killed and numerous villages burnt. I visited some of those villages and saw the destruction of homes and places of worship. Violence has continued, and as recently as 18th November, riots erupted in Kazaure in Jigawa State. Out of 11 churches, nine have been razed to the ground and the other two completely vandalized. Two people were killed and 5,000 displaced, some of them taking refuge in Kano.*
>
> *The implications of these conflicts, which are associated with the imposition of Shari'a law, spread far beyond Nigeria. It is often argued by those who promote Shari'a law that it will not affect non-Muslims. But that claim is disproved by, for example, a current case in Bauchi State, where 11 Christian nurses have been dismissed from their posts in a federal hospital for refusing to accept the Islamic dress code as it violates their professional and human rights. Their case has been upheld in the secular court, but the local administration has refused to re-employ them. I met these nurses on Monday and heard how they are suffering as a result of their unemployment. Many can no longer afford to send their children to school, while some do not have enough money to feed their families.*
>
> *That is just one example of the fundamental problems associated with the incompatibility of some aspects of Shari'a law with the principles enshrined in the*

Universal Declaration of Human Rights, such as equality before the law and the freedom to choose and change religion. For example, under Shari'a law, there is no equality before the law between men and women or between Muslims and non-Muslims, and there is no freedom for Muslims to change religion without incurring the risk of the death penalty for apostasy.

It is issues such as these which underpin the resistance to Shari'a law in many parts of Nigeria, resulting in the conflicts which over the years have been responsible for the deaths of thousands and massive destruction of property. The stability of Nigeria, and President Obasanjo's commitment to democracy and a secular constitution, is vital to the stability of West Africa and beyond. Can the Minister indicate ways in which Her Majesty's Government are assisting or may further assist President Obasanjo to fulfil these very important commitments? They are important for Nigeria and important for Africa ...

Iyasco Taru: A Saint and a Martyr

In her collection of stories, *Cox's Book of Modern Saints and Martyrs*, Caroline Cox shares the account of a modern hero who has left behind a legacy of courage, representative of the powerful faith of Nigeria's Christians. As we've seen, in February 2000, more than 2,000 people were killed in religious unrest in Kaduna, Nigeria. One of those killed was Rev. Iyasco Taru. Here are excerpts from his story.

Rev. Taru was ordained in 1994 as a minister in the Church of the Brethren in Nigeria, and his first posting was in Abuja, the fast-growing capital of Nigeria, where he and his family stayed until 2000.

According to Mrs Rebecca Paul Gadazama, who has compiled a record of Rev. Taru's life, he was transferred to pastor the church in Badarawa Kaduna on 1

January 2000, moving his wife and five children to Kaduna that February. Mrs Gadazama writes:

> *On 20 February there was a crisis all over Kaduna. The next day some Moslem militants marched to Rev. Iyasco Taru's church. They killed all his chickens and turkeys. The militants kept coming and going, considering what to do with Iyasco, his family and church properties. A Moslem neighbour did all he could to stop them from harming the church. The next day the church was set ablaze ... Iyasco did not leave 'the House of God on fire', as he put it. He kept encouraging his family and those around the burning church with the Word of God, referring to what was happening as the fulfilment of the Scriptures.*

Early the next day, Ivasco's wife insisted that they leave, since the church and their home had been destroyed. By that time the militants were going after him and his family, so Iyasco took them to shelter in a church member's house. But the militants came after him, setting the house on fire and slaughtering its owners in front of Iyasco. When the militants turned on Iyasco, he and his four sons were separated from his wife, Benedictta, and their daughter.

"The man and boys were for the kill," writes Mrs Gadazama. "But the Lord stepped in and the leaders of that particular group of militants said women and children were not to be killed. This statement narrowly saved Shalom, the youngest son, who was just about to be hacked down. As he was pushed away, he was telling them about the love of the Lord Jesus Christ. This infuriated the militants more."

Benedictta's abiding memory is of her husband being led away – still telling his attackers about the living, saving grace of Jesus. Benedictta took her surviving children to the military barracks but realized that Shalom was missing. She went in search of her husband and son when the carnage was at its peak. Later, the next day, Shalom was found running among the dead. His father was slaughtered – his body, and the big Bible he was clinging to, were found in a gutter not very far from the church. The bodies of Iyasco and eight fellow believers were retrieved from a mass burial and Badarawa's Catholic priest gave them a Christian burial.

Local Christians ensured that Benedictta and her children were re-housed, but for her life will never be the same. She misses her husband and cannot forget the sight of him being led away to be slaughtered: "His message about the living and saving grace of Jesus at his point of death are still very loud in her ears," writes Mrs Gadazama.

Benedictta's hope is that Iyasco's martyrdom will cause many – including those who murdered him – to turn to Jesus as a result of this message of grace. She prays that her children will pick up their father's Bible, dust it off and follow in his footsteps.

(Excerpt taken from *Cox's Book of Modern Saints and Martyrs*, Continuum Books: London, 2006, p. 115.

Used by permission)

SUDAN

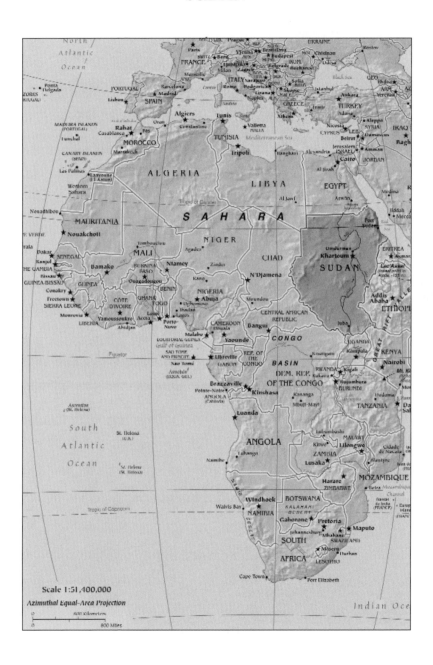

CHAPTER EIGHT

Sudan – Front Line against Islamists

In the dry season, when towering clouds, drenching rains and flash floods are just a memory, Sudan looks very different from the air. From horizon to horizon, much of the south is a vast, flat savannah, with the shadows of former rivers etched into the cracked soil. The terrain is harsh and empty. It was once the domain of lions, leopards and gazelles before years of war and famine caused anything alive to be devoured. Today much of Southern Sudan is a desolate wilderness, bereft of natural wildlife.

The "Land of the Blacks", as the Arabs call Sudan, is the largest nation in Africa. It is the size of Britain, France, Germany, Italy, Belgium, Holland, Spain and Sweden combined; its population, according to a July 2006 estimate was 42,350,000. Muslim Arabs dominate the northern two-thirds, while black African Christians and animists form the majority of the population in the south. It is between North and South, Arab and non-Arab, that Sudan's fault lines lie. The country has been at war with itself for all but eleven of the years since gaining independence on 1 January 1956, when the Republic of Sudan was officially established.

In 1989 an Islamist military regime took power by coup, declaring war against all who oppose it. Its objectives are the Islamization of those who are not already Muslims and the arabization of the African peoples. Resistance to this regime has embroiled the country in a protracted and bitter conflict, in which 2 million perished and 4 million were displaced before the war moved on to Darfur, where more people have perished than in the 2004 tsunami.

The Sudanese People's Liberation Army (SPLA), led by the US-educated and Fort Benning-trained Colonel John Garang de Mabior, held its ground for two decades until peace talks in 2002–2004 led to the Naivasha peace treaty, signed in January 2005. This treaty gave autonomy to Southern Sudan for six years, to be followed by a referendum for independence. John Garang was sworn in as Sudan's vice-president on 9 July 2005, second only to his long-time enemy, President Omar el-Bashir. Garang and Bashir had begun to forge a power-sharing government between the North and the South, which would elevate Garang's SPLA to a status equal to that of Bashir's Sudanese military.

John Garang died in a helicopter crash while returning from Uganda to Southern Sudan just three weeks after being sworn into office.

Meanwhile, the conflict in Darfur, Sudan, which flared up in 2003, displaced another 2 million Sudanese and cost 400,000 more people their lives. The only good thing that can be said for the Darfur crisis is that it has finally turned the world's eyes toward Sudan's agony.

Along with other largely ignored Christian human rights advocates, Baroness Cox was hard at work in Sudan long before the Darfur tragedy became headline news. By that time she had embarked on dozens of dangerous, illicit missions to Southern Sudan, the Nuba Mountains, the Southern Blue Nile and the eastern lands inhabited by the Beja people. She also made one official visit to the Sudanese capital, Khartoum, to hear the regime leadership's version of events.

Encountering Turabi and his Regime

In December 1992, Lady Cox described the state of Sudan's abused population vividly in the House of Lords, and made a plea for Britain to honour its historic obligations to the Sudanese. "The people feel forgotten and betrayed by the rest of the world," she told her peers. "I hope that we in Britain will not fail them in their hour of need." That debate in the House of Lords lasted two hours and 27 minutes. And watching the proceedings from the gallery, with increasing discomfort, were the Sudanese Ambassador and a handful of other Embassy of Sudan representatives.

"If looks could kill," Caroline recalls, "I most certainly would not be alive today."

After the debate, Cox was invited to the Sudanese Embassy to hear about the many good and praiseworthy things that were being done by the Khartoum government. She gladly agreed to the Embassy meeting, but as it dragged on she managed to interrupt what she later described as a monologue of self-congratulation to invite herself to Northern Sudan. She wanted to see for herself if what was being said was true.

In July 1993 Caroline Cox flew into the capital of Sudan with a small team that included Adam Kelliher, a cameraman from Frontline News. Their first day in Khartoum coincided with an indoor gathering to mark the fourth anniversary of the military regime's coup and ascent to power. On the balcony at the rear of the Hall of Friendship, a group of Mujahedin were shouting Islamic chants. A bearded, white-robed imam, brandishing a great sword, led the assembled crowd in a rallying cry for holy war. All in attendance were urged to respond to the cry of the jihadis, to close ranks and reduce their country's fragmentation.

The spirit of jihad was also on parade at the Hussein Ben Ali Popular Defence Force training ground, where white-uniformed, Kalashnikov-carrying Mujahedin marched up and down, chanting in Arabic, "There is only one God and Mohammed is his prophet," and "We are soldiers of Allah." The crowd was reminded that those who gave their lives in the Holy War would become *shu'hada* – martyrs – assured by the

Koran of being rewarded with innumerable sensual delights in Paradise.

"We noticed," Caroline wrote in her notes, "that the virtually compulsory militia requires all its members, be they Muslims, Christians or animists, to sing Islamic chants. The pledge of the government to intensify its programme of Islamization is a cause of great concern to Sudan's non-Muslims."

A meeting was arranged with the leading figure of Sudan's National Islamic Front, Dr Hassan al-Turabi, who courteously received the group in the wood-panelled reception room of his home. When they were settled into plush leather sofas and had been offered tea and cool drinks, Dr Turabi, the Speaker of the Sudanese Parliament, began a monologue. A slight figure behind black-rimmed glasses and a close-cropped grizzled white beard, he spoke at length, using his hands for emphasis, and smiling reassuringly. But the meeting was less than convivial. "He just opened his mouth and out flowed non-stop propaganda," Caroline Cox noted.

Her anger mounting, she began to challenge his assertions. She suspected that many of his visitors would not be familiar with the complexities of the situation in Sudan and might accept his propaganda unquestioningly. The more he persisted, the more she interrupted, challenging the untruths in his spiel. Dr Turabi did not find the novelty amusing; the smile vanished and his face grew darker as the atmosphere chilled. When it dawned on Dr Turabi that this exchange was being filmed, he became angrier still, and he abruptly terminated the interview. All courtesies were suspended as Cox and her colleagues were unceremoniously ushered out of his house.

Sudan's Notorious "Peace Camps"

On that same journey, Caroline Cox visited refugee camps in the North and the Nuba Mountains, a range some 300 miles south of El-Obeid, rising 1,370 metres above the surrounding plains. The mountains are inhabited by people from the Nuba tribes, many of whom were being held in refugee centres that bore a striking resemblance to concentration camps.

Conditions in the camps were appalling. An atmosphere of lethargy and demoralization was pervasive. The people Cox interviewed reported that they had been forced into the camps after government troops had attacked their homes and villages, burned their houses and crops, destroyed their waterholes and left them with nothing. Short of death by thirst or starvation, their only option was the so-called Peace Camps.

Foreign non-governmental organizations (NGOs) were denied access to the camps, and a propaganda campaign had been launched by Khartoum against the NGOs. With a ban on humanitarian missions, Western relief aid could be distributed only by Islamic organizations, which had sole rights to operate in the camps. In Khartoum churches were permitted a small share in the distribution of aid, but in the Nuba Mountains camps, and elsewhere in Southern Sudan, rations were distributed only to those who were willing to convert to Islam. To obtain food and medicine, many of the displaced said they were ordered to renounce their Christian names and adopt Islamic ones. Caroline Cox called it "the politics of hunger".

She recalls how, on several occasions, she encountered people starving and dying of treatable diseases, who could have gone to Government of Sudan health clinics or feeding centres but refused to do so. They asserted that they were Christians and would prefer to die as Christians than convert to Islam in order to obtain life-saving food and medicine. One picture is etched on Caroline Cox's heart: a young, blind, virtually naked mother holding an infant in the last stages of dying from starvation. The mother explained that she would not go to a government clinic or feeding centre, as she would not convert to Islam. Caroline Cox later reflected, "It would be a tough call to sacrifice one's own life for one's faith. To sacrifice your child must be the ultimate anguish – but that is the price people are prepared to pay on the front line of faith in Sudan."

Cox's visits to Sudan continued over the next few months, all conducted without official permission and all involving illegal entry into areas of the country designated "No-Fly Zones" by the Khartoum regime. It was their policy to carry out military offensives against innocent civilians while simultaneously closing those combat zones to the United Nations-led Operation Lifeline Sudan and all the major aid organizations working under the UN umbrella. Consequently, no one could provide aid for the government's victims, or witness the atrocities it was perpetrating, or tell the world what it was doing. It was in these areas that Caroline Cox and her colleagues saw the raw and ruthless brutality of Khartoum's Islamist National Islamic Front, a regime that was never elected but continues to be recognized as the Government of Sudan.

Wherever possible, Caroline Cox met leaders of the opposition groups, who, judging by the votes cast at the annulled election, represented some 90 per cent of the Sudanese people.

In 1994, the year that a new government offensive sent 100,000 South Sudanese refugees fleeing into Uganda, Lady Cox visited Dr John Garang. One of his principal disputes with the North concerned the introduction of Islamic law. He dismissed Dr Turabi's insistence that Shari'a law would not be applied to the South. "It is impossible to exempt the South from the supreme laws of the land," he explained to Baroness Cox. "The NIF will not accept a secular state; we will not accept an Islamic state."

By June 1994, the situation was deteriorating rapidly. Severe fighting had led to the evacuation of 80,000 from the relief camps. Most NGOs had been forced to quit, and the food lifeline was severed. In Mayen Abun, in the Bahr el-Ghazal region, people and cattle were starving. In the previous year, 90 per cent of the local crops had been destroyed by drought. The rains had held off from July to April. Now the seed had shrivelled and blown away. Malnutrition was rife, along with malaria, TB, pneumonia and diarrhoea. Even leprosy was making a comeback; and it was only the beginning of the hungry season. There were four months to go before harvest, and already most of the roots and grasses had been eaten.

A few yards from the airstrip where her small aircraft had landed, Caroline came across two of hunger's victims. A man of around 50 had walked for more than five days to find food, and had found nothing. Meanwhile, an 18-year-old girl lay in the shade of a thorn tree, dying of starvation and TB. Her skin was stretched tightly across her skull. She was beyond the capacity to digest food and there was no medicine for her. She had only hours to live. Caroline did what she could, taking the time to provide a drink of water, to say a quiet prayer with the two victims, to hold their hands and touch their foreheads, to somehow comfort them in their dying moments. They were so weak they could not lift their limbs, yet they responded with wide smiles of appreciation. The next morning, when Caroline returned to visit them, they were both dead.

That same day Lady Cox encountered Akel Deng, a young widow who was naked to her waist apart from a locket. Her husband had died an hour earlier. She knelt in silence on a mat of reeds beside the dead body, her face a mask of grief and resignation, her hands lifted to God. For half an hour, Caroline knelt alongside Akel, her arm embracing the bereaved woman. Sharing grief across a vast cultural divide, the two quietly cried and prayed together.

Later on, Akel's husband was laid to rest in the red soil. Akel tried to comfort one wailing child while another hid behind a tree, unable to face what had happened to his father. "My heart broke over the extent of the suffering and for the fact that so much of it is forgotten," Cox later said. "The rest of the world doesn't know and doesn't seem to care."

Father Benjamin Madol Akot, a Roman Catholic priest,

thanked Caroline for choosing to open her eyes to their need. "We have felt deserted, even betrayed, by Christians in the West. We have suffered for 27 years, seeking help, but it doesn't materialize."

If possible, things were even worse in the Nuba Mountains. There were some 3 million Nuba, from a variety of tribes. These were black Africans, most of whom spoke Arabic as their first language. Some 40 per cent were Muslim; up to 30 per cent were Christian and the rest were animist (some local community leaders maintain that the majority of Nubans are Christians). Yet Muslims, Christians and animists alike were being systematically ousted from their homes by government forces. Around a quarter of a million were living in territory nominally under SPLA control while many more had been displaced.

The church in the Nuba Mountains had been cut off from the outside world for more than a decade, though their problems had begun even earlier, in 1962, when the military regime of General Abboud had expelled all missionaries from the country. There were few clergy, yet the church had continued to thrive, kept alive by a few priests and the dedicated, courageous catechists. They made up for their lack of education with zeal, braving snake and insect bites and malaria to travel around the country performing their Christian duties.

The Nuba Anglican priests had nothing, so Caroline Cox and her team gave them Bibles and service books, and even handed over their own wristwatches. In return, the hungry priests gave them a hen, which Caroline entrusted back to them with a smile, promising to return to share a meal of freshly laid eggs at some later date. "You are the first Christians who have come to encourage us," said the Rev. Barnabas, the Anglican Chairman of the Nuba New Sudan Council of Churches. "We will never forget you."

A Town Called Nyamlell

During the mid-1990s, Caroline got to know Sudan pretty well. But nothing had prepared her for what she was to find in Nyamlell. Adjacent to the town was an airstrip that the government had closed to aid deliveries. As usual, all entry was forbidden to NGOs. Caroline and her team ignored the prohibition and no sooner had their Cessna Caravan touched down on the landing strip, whipping up clouds of dust, than people appeared from all directions to greet them, relief written large on their faces. "Thank God you've come!" announced Commissioner Aleu Akechak Jok, a clean-shaven, bespectacled man in Western clothes. He was a judge who had given up his practice in Khartoum to be with his people in their war. "We thought the world had completely forgotten us."

Nyamlell had not recovered from a brutal attack by jihadi warriors in March 1995, two months before. Encouraged and equipped by the government of Khartoum, some 2,000 well-armed men had descended on the village on horseback. They were Arabs from the Rizeigat and Misseriya tribes, along with Government of Sudan Army soldiers and members of the Popular Defence Forces (PDF). They killed 82 villagers, mainly men, and wounded many more, leaving the old for dead. They torched houses, seized livestock, stripped the village of every personal possession – even cooking pots – and rounded up the cattle. Herded behind the horses, with the cattle, were 282 women and children. Nyamlell's airstrip was one of those closed by Khartoum. Not only did this prevent outside aid from reaching the villagers, but, again, it kept outsiders' eyes from seeing what had happened.

By the time Caroline Cox arrived, eight weeks had passed since the militia's assault. In the blackened ruins of their *tukuls*, remaining townsfolk lined up to bear witness. Others emerged from the bush, having walked for hours to describe similar attacks on their own villages. "We were armed with spears and they were armed with Kalashnikovs," reported

Garang Amok Mou, who had lost seven brothers – four killed and three captured. "My brothers were killed because they were holding spears to try to rescue their families, and they were mown down by gunfire. We cannot possibly defend our people when we only have traditional weapons to fight against well-armed militias with automatic rifles."

Abuk Marou Keer is blind. She appeared one afternoon wearing a tattered grey top over a pastel-coloured skirt. She described how she had been hauled to her feet and almost strangled by her beads. She and her children were taken away with the other captives, beaten, then forced to walk. She stumbled sightlessly behind the horses, struggling to carry property that had been looted by her captors. Their destination was an agricultural labour camp at Araith, 18 miles to the north. "Four male captives were murdered by the Arabs," she explained to Caroline Cox, "and many women were raped." She was among them. "The soldiers said this was retaliation for the death of one of their leaders in the raid against Nyamlell…we were also forced to grind grain from sunrise to sunset. All we had to eat was the leftover waste from grinding. We were beaten, sometimes with whips, but they left our hands untied."

Abuk Keer tried her best to describe the desperation she felt. Because she is blind, she had been abandoned when two children were taken away as slaves. She quietly explained, "In Africa, if you are blind, your children are your eyes. I am blind; I have lost my children. I will die. I have been told by Arab traders that my children are alive and they know where they are. But they need money to buy their freedom – and I don't have any money or anything left after this raid."

Caroline Cox and her colleagues provided the money Abuk needed to pay Arab traders the price of her children's freedom. When they returned to Nyamllel a few months later, a very happy Abuk Keer was sitting in her home with a radiant smile, exclaiming, "I am so happy my children have come home! If I weren't blind, I could dance all night. We are together as a family. That is all that matters."

It was in Nyamlell that Baroness Cox first became an eyewitness to slave trading. It was there that she heard testimony after testimony that women and children were herded behind the horses after an Islamist raid, taken captive to be sold into slavery, usually in Northern Sudan, but sometimes transported to homes or armies in the Middle East and Europe.

In his 1995 "Interim Report on the Situation of Human Rights in the Sudan," United Nations Special Rapporteur Gaspar Biro wrote of an "alarming increase in the number of reports" from a wide variety of sources of cases of slavery in Sudan. He wrote of an incident in Aweil "where PDF troops ... took thousands of cattle and abducted some 500 women and 150 children between five and twelve years of age ... taken to Al-Islamiyya, an Islamic non-governmental organization active in the field of education, while the government claims that they are displaced children. Big boys are distributed as workers ... they work in the fields or as servants ... Girls become concubines or wives, mainly of soldiers and PDF members in northern Sudan ... Dinka boys as young as 11 or 12 years reportedly receive military training and are sent by the government of Sudan to fight the war in Southern Sudan ... The Special Rapporteur cannot but conclude that the ... traffic in and sale of children and women, slavery, servitude, forced labour and similar practices are taking place with the knowledge of the government of Sudan ... The manifest passivity of the government of Sudan ... after years of reporting ... leads to the conclusion that abductions, slavery and institutions and practices similar to slavery are carried out by persons acting under the authority and with the tacit approval of the government of Sudan."

Gaspar Biro was later banned from Sudan. At around the same time, Caroline Cox stepped into the nightmare and defiantly made illicit trips to Nyamlell and other destinations with foreign media correspondents in tow, meeting slave traders, redeeming hundreds of Sudanese slaves, setting them free, and making sure every transaction was recorded on videotape for all the world to see. It was a controversial effort, to be sure. And Cox did not look upon it lightly. She described to Andrew Boyd her reaction to the atrocity of slave trading:

> *The feelings are so deep and so complicated; it's hard to verbalize them. Immense, deep grief. If you talk to a mother whose children are currently slaves, what do you say? There aren't any words to describe it. Deep anger. And this is part of a systematic policy, being pursued and encouraged by a government that is sitting in Khartoum. It makes me feel intense anger and a passionate commitment to try to do something about it, to try and expose it, to try to get it stopped, to try to get anyone who is at the moment a slave, set free.*

In response to criticisms that she and her colleagues were "encouraging the slave trade", Cox defends the policy by pointing out that those who make this criticism do not understand the situation. "This slavery is not economic. It is a weapon of war. This enslavement would take place on this massive scale, whether or not we ever redeemed a single slave. And we believe there is a moral mandate to set the slave free. Let those who criticize us in London, Nairobi or New York come and see the reality – and then they will be in a position to judge for themselves if they could leave women and children in slavery with a clear conscience."

Four Women from Aweil

In the area surrounding the southern Sudanese city of Yei, Baroness Cox interviewed a number of women who survived the brutal attacks of the Khartoum-backed militias, violent incursions that decimated their homes and villages. One woman, Monica, said of her village, "Aweil is desolate: the cattle are gone; the durra (staple food) is gone. We are crying to God: 'If you really love us, look after us! We are dying of hunger. We are suffering terribly.'"

Bakita is also from Aweil, and except for her two small children she is the sole surviving member of her family. Her parents died during the war, as did her uncle and aunt. Her brother was forcibly taken to the Arab area and lost his mind as a result of the abuses he suffered. Bakita herself fell ill after the trauma she experienced, and at times she has feared that she, too, might lose her mind. She said everyone in Aweil was in a similar situation. "The fields are empty because many have died or run away. There is nothing to eat or drink. Many are sick. Others have gone mad in the harsh prevailing conditions. Most people have nothing to eat."

"And we have little to drink either," added another Aweil villager named Regina. "The people drink from (polluted) rivers because there is no other source of water. There is great suffering in Aweil. Some of us are barefooted, some have no clothes, some have no proper homes. However, the biggest problem is water."

Mary, a fourth villager, explained to Caroline Cox, "Faith alone sustains us. We have been asking God what we can do." In Mary's view the two main problems are a lack of water – people have to travel as far as eight miles to find it – and the fact that there is no grinding machine. The area is isolated and devastated. "We are starting from zero," Mary concluded.

Yei, Southern Sudan

The 2005 Comprehensive Peace Agreement (CPA) led to the establishment of a Government of National Unity, an entity designed to bring together previously warring factions in Sudan's North and South. However, the CPA has created many problems for the South of the country. It has not provided fair and effective representation in key government positions for Southerners, nor has it assured justice in the distribution of Sudan's potentially abundant natural resources, particularly in the sharing of oil revenues.

The long civil war left a legacy of massive devastation, destruction of essential infrastructure, and a vast humanitarian crisis. A generation of young people in many areas has been deprived of the most basic needs, including education, because of the fighting, and there is a severe and widespread lack of adequate health care.

Today local communities are trying to re-establish their own facilities and to provide education for the "lost generation" and health care for the countless numbers of citizens currently suffering and dying without access to treatment. There is an urgent need for more primary and preventive health care and health education in towns and rural communities.

In 2006, Caroline Cox led a team into Yei because it epitomized so many of the problems of Southern Sudan. The town had been the focus of intense battles as it changed hands to and fro between the NIF and the SPLM. For several years it also sustained such repeated and heavy bombardment that it was largely devastated and the people still suffer from the war's repercussions. Bishop Elias Taban and other community leaders met Caroline Cox and her colleagues and accompanied them to an orphanage, a clinic, a hospital under construction, and a college that provides teacher training and theological education. "We were deeply impressed by the love, warmth and standard of care at the orphanage," Cox reported. She continued:

> The nurses at the clinic were also impressive in their professional competence. We discussed with them the urgent need for more community nurses and midwives to provide clinical care in outlying areas. As the clinic serves a large catchment area with a diameter of approximately 50 miles, many in need of treatment may be unable to obtain it. Some treatment could usefully be provided by mobile medical units, but there is also a great need for more preventive health care and health education, especially in the more remote areas.
>
> The teacher-training college, together with the

theological college, will make a valuable contribution to alleviating the problems of shortfall in the provision of education and church ministry.

We were also pleased to see a Women's Empowerment Programme in Yei, as this may obviously help women economically, socially and personally to make their contribution more effectively in the development of Southern Sudan. The significance of this initiative is illustrated by the experiences of a number of women from Aweil who had come especially to Yei to participate in it. Their stories demonstrate the kind of suffering which they, and countless others like them, have endured, and are still enduring, in their part of Southern Sudan.

During that 2006 visit to Sudan, Baroness Cox also heard expressions of deep concern from some community leaders over the rapid increase in Islamic aid organizations. These leaders feared that such organizations cynically use the humanitarian crisis in Sudan to introduce the militant Wahhabist form of Islam. President El Bashir's announcement (in Juba, February 2006) of the government's intention to pour money into the South for humanitarian purposes was welcomed by some. But others saw it as part of an Islamic agenda. They expressed concern that Islamic NGOs often use relief supplies as a means to promote conversion to Islam. "Such a conversion," one leader said, shaking his head, "is a one-way street."

Once people have agreed to become Muslim – even if they do so only as a means of getting food, water, medical care or other necessities – it is difficult and dangerous to "un-convert". Under Shari'a law, such recanting is considered "apostasy", an offence that carries with it, at best, the likelihood of rejection by family and friends, but also the very real possibility of the death penalty. One community leader said, "The NIF will achieve its Islamist agenda through winning in peace what it failed to achieve by war. It is now putting the millions and millions of dollars it spent on the war into winning the peace through providing aid. This aid is conditional and a tool for conversion to Islam."

Some community leaders have in their possession a document spelling out a budget and proposals for the Islamization of Southern Sudan. It details teacher training colleges, schools, school meals, uniforms and (Koranic) textbooks; hospitals, medicines, nurses' uniforms, and so on. The total budget, $29 million, has been sent to supporters in Saudi Arabia and other Islamist leaders and is pouring into Southern Sudan.

Christian leaders deeply regretted the absence of comparable Christian resources. They point out that Islam is operating strategically while Western Christianity is "asleep" and rapidly losing ground – spiritually, economically, politically and militarily.

Among Sudan's Lepers

In January 2007, Baroness Cox returned to Sudan. The primary purpose of her visit to Chotburo in Eastern Upper Nile was to help to investigate the existence of suspected but as yet unofficially reported cases of leprosy. She explains, "The humanitarian organization Servant's Heart has been working in Longachok County since May 2001, with projects in the fields of health care and education. In these areas in Eastern Upper Nile, there have been reports of cases of suspected leprosy in the Payams of Daja, Chotburo, and Wudier." She intended to help establish a treatment programme for this part of Sudan, if cases of leprosy were found.

During the ten-day visit to Longachok County, 18 people were identified with signs and symptoms suggestive of leprosy. Later, in Yei Hospital Leprosy Centre, the staff agreed with the field diagnosis on the basis of the photographs and case studies. There were also many reports of other people in the localities who were suspected by other villagers of having leprosy. However, as Cox's visit took place during the dry season, many of these possible sufferers were on the move with their cattle in search of water, and were therefore unavailable for diagnosis.

Baroness Cox wrote:

> *We are grateful to the clinical staff at the Centre who looked at our photographs of suspected cases of leprosy in our locations in Eastern Upper Nile. They immediately and unequivocally agreed with the diagnosis. They introduced us to some of their 17 patients, demonstrating similar symptoms and signs. They also described their treatment policies for different forms of leprosy.*
>
> *Their emphatic endorsement of our evidence of the existence of leprosy in the cases we had identified gave us the confidence to forward our draft reports to the relevant authorities ...*

As they looked into the possible outbreak of leprosy in the Yei area, Cox and her colleagues also identified myriad other health care concerns – not as dramatic as leprosy, perhaps, but dangerous and deadly nonetheless.

Visiting other locations, in Central Equatoria, she reports:

> *In the few days before we arrived, ten people had succumbed to meningitis. In fact the day before we came, the local policeman had died of this illness. Many pregnant women with complications in childbirth have died, together with their babies, because the only way to take them to hospital is by bicycle on a devastated road which is virtually impassable in the rainy season.*
>
> *The scale and range of diseases rampant in the local community, which could be treated if the hospital could function, include malaria, typhoid fever, worms (including hookworms and tapeworms), TB, STDs, HIV/AIDS, leprosy, sleeping sickness, measles, chicken pox, whooping cough, cholera, diarrhoea and gastric ulcers.*
>
> *But at present, although the local clinical assistant*

> *has a microscope, he does not have any of the equipment to enable him to use it.*
>
> *Such is the tragic predicament of the people in these parts of Southern Sudan. The present population in the hospital's surrounding area is approximately 25,000 and the existing problems are being exacerbated by an influx of people moving into the area, from even more impoverished places.*
>
> *Michael, the nurse, told us:*
>
> *"Just recently, we have had outbreaks of measles and meningitis – we have seen so many cases. We sent some to Yei, but some died on the way, because we do not have adequate transport. If we had transport, this could make a difference. Please help us."*

The only facility available in Logo, an area adjacent to Yei, is a simple mud-brick building with a leaking roof. Although it is only about 20 km from Yei, the poor condition of the roads makes it virtually impossible to transport ill and injured people there. Also, pregnant mothers who experience problems in childbirth often die on the way to the hospital, as they have to travel by bicycle on the very bumpy roads. According to the midwife, two out of every ten babies die during or soon after delivery.

In early 2007, there was one midwife to serve the entire area, and a clinical assistant who visits only once a week – on Tuesdays. The Bishop is working with the local community to rebuild an adjacent building that is now derelict, having been destroyed in the war. Meanwhile, the present situation is bleak. As a local community elder remarked dryly to Baroness Cox, "Illnesses do not wait until Tuesdays to come."

The Quest for a Strong Southern Sudan

Her Excellency Rebecca N. de Mabior, widow of John Garang, the former vice-president of Sudan, is a long-standing friend of Caroline Cox. They were reunited in February 2007. A tall, elegant and impressive woman, Ms De Mabior expressed not only personal grief over her bereavement, but also grief for the loss of a man whose vision and commitment had contributed so much to the birth of "New Sudan". Despite her personal loss, she emphasized her determination, and the commitment of those around her, to do everything possible to ensure that John Garang's vision will ultimately be realized. She is determined that those now responsible for Southern Sudan will prove themselves worthy of the price he paid for their freedom.

Violent disturbances have taken place since the signing of the peace treaty. There was a massacre near Juba in October 2006, and just over a month later, in late November, conflict erupted at Malakal, in which least 150 people were killed and 400 to 500 were wounded in clashes between the Sudanese Army and former SPLA rebels. Such incidents are believed by many to have been instigated in the North by those who intend to undermine Southern Sudan's leadership.

Also alarming are widespread reports of mass immigration into the South by newcomers from regions in east Africa. This, of course, places great strain on an already devastated society which lacks adequate resources for its own people. But this problem is compounded by fears that some of these new immigrants may represent a militant and strategic Islamic agenda, intent upon changing the religious and ethnic composition of the South's demographic structure.

As we have seen, the people of Southern Sudan have traditionally been Christians, "moderate" Muslims and traditional believers. They have generally been committed to tolerance, living in peaceful co-existence. However, in recent years, the people of the South have been forced to defend not only their land but also their way of life. They have found themselves forming a front line against militant Islam, a religious totalitarian system that seeks to overrun Southern Sudan and beyond.

Baroness Cox raised this matter with the British

government on 30 January 2006. "My Lords, I am grateful to my noble friend Lord Alton for once again bringing the tragedy of Darfur to our attention. He has cited the chilling details of what is happening there so comprehensively that not much more information needs to be added." She continued:

> *I emphasize my strong support for his request for targeted sanctions, such as no-fly zones or the denial of visas to official representatives of the regime in Khartoum. I also support his plea for a greater disinvestment campaign. Such a campaign, implemented by official bodies and other influential groups such as churches, helped to bring an end to apartheid. I often wonder why we have been so slow to effect such a policy against the brutal regime in Khartoum, which benefits from international recognition and foreign investment even as it continues to kill its own people.*
>
> *I therefore ask the Minister why Her Majesty's Government gave official invitations and red-carpet treatment to personnel such as the chairman of the Khartoum Chamber of Commerce. What will it take for Her Majesty's Government to refrain from doing business with those in Khartoum perpetrating their genocidal policies, with 2 million dead and 4 million displaced before the Darfur conflict, which has killed more people than the tsunami?*
>
> *As my noble friend indicated, I shall focus on some of the grave implications of the fall-out of the war in Darfur for the rest of Sudan. While resources and media attention are focused almost exclusively on Darfur, other dire and dangerous situations go unreported and unaddressed. As my noble friend said, I was in Southern Sudan just ten days ago for nearly two weeks, and saw many of the problems of the aftermath of decades of intense war: a devastated infrastructure of roads and public services such as health care and an urgent need for education for a generation of children denied access to schools, both during the war and today. There is also widespread*

concern that the Government in Khartoum are denying the South the resources needed for reconstruction to create disaffection with the Government of Southern Sudan. They are thereby undermining the peace process by supporting militants and encouraging a process of Islamization through strategic interventions.

The lack of adequate health care was reflected in one of the most horrifying discoveries of our visit. In Eastern Upper Nile, we were surrounded by naked children with severe malnutrition and preventable and treatable diseases who were receiving no treatment. Even more shocking was the discovery of leprosy. We took photographs and case studies to the leprosy centre in Yei, where staff agreed with the diagnosis of leprosy, which is possibly of pandemic proportions in Eastern Upper Nile. In Central Equatoria, we found people dying from other treatable diseases, such as measles and meningitis or from complications in childbirth because of lack of medical care or access to hospital. The problems caused by such acute shortages of essential resources are exacerbated by an influx of refugees from Darfur who, having fled from the horrors there, find further suffering in the devastation and deprivations of the South.

It is also feared that the Government in Khartoum are deliberately and systematically destabilizing the South by supporting militias and instigating recent outbreaks of fighting such as that in Malakal and the massacre outside Juba last October. Moreover, the large-scale immigration of newcomers from East Africa raises fears that some new immigrants represent a militant and strategic Islam which will affect the demographic structure of the South, changing its religious and ethnic composition before the referendum to determine its future, and therefore possibly affecting the outcome of that referendum. The South is in a geographically vulnerable position with Khartoum's influence on every border: there are many al-Qaeda militants in East Africa; on the southern border, the so-called Lord's Resistance Army, which is supported by Khartoum, is sustaining its terrorist policies in Northern Uganda and Southern Sudan, wreaking havoc; the genocidal conflict in Darfur is to the north; and Ethiopian militant rebels, also supported by Khartoum, are destabilizing the eastern borderlands.

The people of Southern Sudan are Christians, Muslims and traditional believers, who have generally lived in peaceful co-existence. However, during recent years, they have been forced to defend a front line against a militant Islam that would overrun Southern Sudan and rapidly spread further. It has been claimed that it is only the resistance by Southern Sudan that is preventing the Islamization of the rest of Africa, down to Cape Town. For that reason there are real fears that the government in Khartoum, having destroyed the way of life of the people of Darfur and left destroyed communities and structures everywhere, will do everything possible to prevent the development of a peaceful, stable, prosperous and democratic South.

Therefore, the challenges confronting the South, such as the provision of adequate resources to rebuild devastated lands and lives, need to be addressed urgently if the peace, which was won at such a price, is not going to be lost in another war or exploited to fulfil an Islamist agenda that could spread not only through Sudan, but far beyond in Africa. I hope that the Minister will reassure the House that Her Majesty's Government are addressing these problems and will not allow the focus on the horrors of Darfur totally to distract attention from the perilous and parlous state of much of the rest of Sudan.

NORTHERN UGANDA

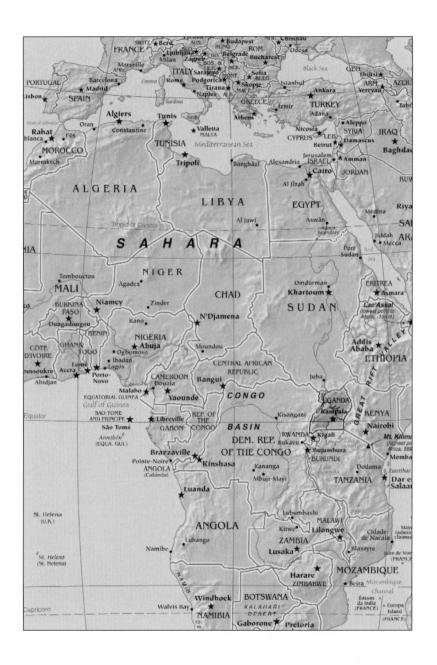

CHAPTER NINE

Northern Uganda – "Terrorists to the Core"

Baroness Cox's powerful defence of the Southern Sudanese people has continued for more than a decade, and she has almost lost count of the times she has visited that war-torn country. However, in February 2006, when she and a group of colleagues returned there, Sudan wasn't their only destination. They also took a hazardous side-trip to Northern Uganda, where yet another conflict is taking an enormous toll on the population. To describe that situation, Lady Cox quotes Olara A. Otunnu, former UN Under-Secretary General and Special Representative for Children in Armed Conflict:

> *The human rights and humanitarian catastrophe unfolding in Northern Uganda is a methodical and comprehensive genocide, conceived and being carried out … An entire society is being systematically destroyed – physically, culturally, emotionally, socially and economically – in full view of the international community. In the sobering words of Father Carlos Rodriguez, a Catholic missionary priest in the region,*
> > *"Everything Acholi (the largest tribe affected in Northern Uganda) is dying."*
> > *Or, as MSF has reported,*
> > *"The extent of suffering is overwhelming … according to international benchmarks, this constitutes an emergency out of control."*
> > *I know of no recent or present situation where all the elements that constitute genocide, under the*

Convention on the Prevention and Punishment of Genocide (1948), have been brought together in such a chillingly comprehensive manner, as in Northern Uganda today.

While most of the Ugandan nation has enjoyed relative peace and security in recent years, the north has been wracked by civil war, caused by the relentless campaign of insurgency waged by the so-called Lord's Resistance Army (LRA). Its ruthless policies have reduced northern areas to a state of devastation: villages have been systematically attacked, property destroyed, and people slaughtered and driven off their lands. Now 95 per cent of the 1.25 million people in the region have been herded into vast concentration-style camps, where they endure dense overcrowding and the lack of adequate water, sanitation, food and other amenities such as health care and education. One thousand people a week die because of the conditions in these camps.

But the most horrifying hallmark of the LRA's insurgency is its systematic abduction of at least 25,000 children; a policy of brutalizing and terrorizing them, and forcing them to fight as soldiers in the LRA against their own people. They are also forced to abduct other children and to abuse them in ways in which they themselves have been maltreated.

For 20 years, the people of Northern Uganda have been subjected to outrageous violations of human rights at the hands of the LRA. Their plight has been complicated by the Ugandan army as it has endeavoured to respond militarily. In recent years there have been reports of atrocities perpetrated on a horrifying scale, especially against children, by the LRA. However, more recently, there have been suggestions that the situation in Northern Uganda is improving and the suffering of the people is consequently being alleviated.

Baroness Cox was asked by representatives of the communities there to visit the region, to help them address the catastrophic situation that continues. The districts of Gulu, Kitgum and Pader were chosen by Caroline Cox's team as destinations (contrary to official advice not to travel there, as the security situation was so high risk) in order to assess current humanitarian needs and the violations of human rights inflicted on the local population – especially on the thousands of children abducted by the LRA. The sites to be visited included camps for displaced people (IDPs) and facilities providing health care and social welfare: night shelters; an orphanage; and a rehabilitation centre for children who had been abducted by the LRA.

Archbishop John Baptist Odama had some meaningful words of greeting for Caroline Cox and her colleagues from HART when they arrived in Gulu, Northern Uganda: "The time for your visit to Northern Uganda," he told them, "is *NOW*." His words reflected a deep and widely-felt concern that the situation there is being reported as "better" or "improved" or "alleviated".

In fact, the situation remains catastrophic. Virtually no villages remain. They have either been destroyed by fighting or abandoned because of LRA attacks, with killings, abductions and looting. Caroline Cox describes one visit to a refugee camp:

> *Ten minutes' drive from the town of Kitgum took us to Labuje camp where we saw people whose lives are reduced, as one young man described it, to living like rats. The huts are so close that one barely finds space for access. The few pit latrines are used by thousands of people. The stench, dirt and a total lack of hygiene create a breeding ground for deadly diseases like diarrhoea, cholera and malaria. Hundreds of empty 20-litre plastic containers are lined up around one borehole waiting to be filled with water; people usually have to wait for no less than five hours to fill these containers. Almost every household lives with at least seven to nine people of different generations packed into a 2-metre-diameter floor space.*
>
> *The LRA's brutal policy of systematic abduction of children has also created the phenomenon of many*

thousands of "Commuter Children" who have to walk to towns every night to the safety provided by night shelters. The shelters can offer no food; the children often sleep on concrete floors without mattresses or blankets; and they leave early in the morning to go to school on empty stomachs.

Yet, as difficult as life is for these children, they are the fortunate ones: they have avoided falling into the hands of the LRA. The most shocking aspect of Lady Cox's visit was learning about the 25,000 to 40,000 children (the numbers are uncertain) who have been abducted and the atrocious experiences to which they are subjected. Many have been killed and their stories will never be known. But a few stories, gathered in interviews by Caroline Cox, seem to be representative of innumerable others. The children describe experiences that are striking in their consistency; these survivors therefore surely speak for thousands of other girls and boys who did not fare so well.

Florence is now 20 years old – she seems much older – but she was just fifteen when she was abducted from Patongo in 2002 and taken to Adak in Sudan. She was forced by the LRA to carry heavy parcels of looted food on her head, and yet even as she walked under the weight of this burden, her arms were bound. And for a week and a half she was fed virtually nothing. Before long, Florence was presented to an LRA commander to be his "wife". Florence was also trained to become a soldier and taught to kill. She confessed to Lady Cox that, before long, she had become "just like" those who abducted her.

Florence fought her way through five bloody missions, and she was given the task of taking other captive children into Southern Sudan, treating them as she had been treated along the way. "I became wild; I didn't care about killing and I possibly became worse than them," she confessed. "If I had met my mother and father I would have killed them, too. I acted like someone who is deranged. I don't know how many people I have killed. And yet despite all the brainwashing, killing and becoming like the LRA, and even trusting them, still I wanted to escape and finally I did so during an operation."

Today Florence lives with her grandmother, and is responsible for the care of her four surviving siblings. She is desperate for education, but has no money to pay for it.

Daniel was also from Patongo. He was 20 years old at the time, and remained in captivity for a year. When he was first captured, he was tied up for three months, given barely enough food for survival, and frequently beaten. Several of those captured with him died. Daniel was taken to Juba (in Southern Sudan) where the infamous LRA Commander Otti subjected him and others to a brutal form of training. After being taught how to handle guns, the young captives were divided into groups and ordered to engage in gun fights with live ammunition. One by one, they killed each other. Those who survived were conscripted into the army.

The survivors were led by Brigadier Banya into Northern Uganda, where they were once again ordered to use their guns in attacks. Daniel commented to Lady Cox that they were not indoctrinated with any ideology – they were taught only brutality. On 7 April 2002, Daniel received orders to participate in a raid on his own village. Their group was divided into small units, which were to attack from all sides. Once Daniel realized he was being sent into his hometown, he thought he might be able to flee. He took civilian clothes along, and in the course of the fighting managed to escape.

But this courageous young man quickly discovered that both his parents had been killed by the LRA and that his three brothers and one sister had all been abducted. Daniel believes his brothers are dead but he doesn't know what has happened to his sister. Today his goal is to somehow complete his education, but, like everyone else in Northern Uganda, he has little hope of doing so.

Charles, 19, wide-eyed and nervous, explained that he is from Lukole and was abducted in 2003. He was attending school about 20 miles away from home, and as his father drove him to class one morning their car was ambushed. Charles' father was killed trying to escape and Charles was abducted and marched to Juba on foot. There he began military training, but trouble developed in Juba so they were moved deeper into Sudan.

As they headed back to Uganda, they raided and looted villages. On one occasion, when their group captured a Sudanese civilian man along the way, Charles was ordered to kill him – or else he himself would be killed. Once they reached Uganda, their unit, comprising 23 men, was deployed to fight Ugandan soldiers. Only nine of them survived; more were killed in subsequent battles. Charles was in the bush for 18 months with the LRA. Their strategy was to make abduction of children their priority.

"I became wild and didn't care if I killed or not. I have no idea how many I killed in crossfire," Charles told Lady Cox. "The LRA taught us that we would never return home and that, if we did so, we would find our parents dead. 'There is no home for you,' they told me. 'And the only thing you can do is to fight and to overthrow the government of Uganda.' I had to pretend, but I knew it wasn't true. In one confrontation, the fighting was very intense and hot and I was left alone with my gun. I left it to go to the river for a drink and I was taken by Ugandan soldiers."

Alice was abducted from Korolalogi Village in 2002, when she was 16 years old. The LRA attacked early one morning while it was still dark and she and her six roommates were sound asleep. The girls were ordered to carry beans, maize and sorghum for their captors, and forced to walk ten or twelve miles along with hundreds of other captives. Alice watched as one girl collapsed under her burden, unable to take another step. The soldiers split her head open with an axe and left her to die where she fell.

The next morning, naked from the waist up, the girls were paraded in front of the LRA soldiers. Afterwards, in order to frighten them so they wouldn't try to escape, the soldiers beat the young women. Just then Ugandan army helicopters appeared overhead, dropping bombs, and many of the abductees and LRA soldiers were killed. The others scattered across the countryside. Alice and three other girls tried to escape but were re-captured and forced to walk to Sudan. One of the girls, Alice's sister, died of cholera on the way.

When they arrived in Sudan, the remaining girls were distributed among the LRA soldiers. Alice's new "husband's" name was Oyo. He had many other wives and mistreated Alice badly, beating her and demanding that she have sex with him – she had refused to do so, she explained, because she didn't love him. Alice lived in the bush under those conditions for two years; she finally managed to escape one night with another girl who had to leave her two children behind. They walked for two weeks and reached Gulu in January 2006. Although she is now in a safe place, after witnessing so much violence and atrocity Alice is unable to sleep without reliving it all again in terrifying nightmares.

A Gift of Cherished Bible Verses

In her small North London flat, Baroness Cox rushes past a pile of the battered clothing she has worn just weeks before in Sudan and Uganda. Today her attire is far more formal: a businesslike black suit, a white blouse and a pearl necklace. Moving quickly, she settles herself behind the wheel of her car and wends her way through the morning traffic to the Palace of Westminster, where she hurriedly strides into the Peers' Entrance of the House of Lords.

It is 15 March 2006, yet another important day for her. Once again, in her role as "Voice for the Voiceless", she will be addressing her peers in the House of Lords on the subject of Northern Uganda. Once again, she will speak on behalf of the discouraged African community leaders she has recently met, the devastated young men and women she has interviewed, the torched villages she has surveyed, and the shattered families she has been told about.

When her moment arrives, she tucks her brown hair automatically behind her ears and begins to speak her mind to the British government. "My Lords," she begins with a brief smile, "I am most grateful ... for this opportunity to record my concerns about my visit three weeks ago to Northern Uganda, where 95 per cent of the population has been herded into over-crowded camps."

She glances around to see who is in attendance, then focuses on her carefully prepared text and continues:

> We witnessed conditions showing why 1,000 people die every week in those camps. We also met some of the tens of thousands of children who had been abducted by the LRA but who had escaped. Their stories have a chilling consistency, and their voices need to be heard tonight. I give just four examples. Florence, fifteen, was abducted in 2002 and taken to Sudan, given to an LRA commander as his "wife", and trained to become a soldier. She had to fight and take other children into captivity, treating them as she had been treated. She said, "I became wild; I didn't care about killing and I possibly became worse than them. If I had met my mother and father I would have killed them. I acted like someone who is deranged. I don't know how many people I have killed." She has been told that her parents are dead. Of her seven siblings, four were abducted, and the others were killed in battle.
>
> Richard, 22, was abducted in 1999. When he was with the LRA, he was forced to do three things: to rape a women publicly; to kill another abductee with a hoe; and to throw an abductee down a well. He received injuries from being beaten with a bicycle chain – a punishment for taking too long to push the abductee down the well.
>
> Irene, fifteen, was abducted in 2001. The LRA made her kill ten other children. She slashed them open with a panga knife, scooping up the blood and placing it in her

mouth. She has repeated nightmares about the first killing, which occurred at dawn. It was the first time she had to drink human blood.

Monica, 18, was abducted in 2003, taken to Sudan for military training, and given to a commander. She became pregnant and had to give birth with no help at all. She said, "I was just treated like an animal." She had to go to fight in Uganda, carrying her baby with her. Time and again, she has had to kill. She said, "In a battle, one has to kill." During one battle near her village, she met a woman whom she knew, and she asked her to take her child, then 18 months old, because she said that she could no longer carry her baby and her gun.

I cannot continue with this terrible catalogue, but I must ask the Minister what Her Majesty's Government are doing to urge President Museveni to declare Northern Uganda a disaster area. In addition, what are they doing to support international aid organizations to prevent the escalation of suffering and death in the camps, and to offer help to the Ugandan Government to provide the security to enable the people to return to their villages? Finally, what are they doing to encourage the Ugandan Government and international organizations to provide free education for children and young people who have escaped from the LRA? The most frequent cri de coeur *was for education. This is a lost generation; they cannot afford school fees.*

I passionately hope that the Minister will promise that efforts will be made by international organizations to provide the education these young people need to find some healing from the indescribable suffering they have endured.

Caroline Cox returned to Northern Uganda in October 2006, to initiate a programme that would provide care for infant orphans in one of the camps for people forced from their lands by the LRA violence.

The situation was a little less tense, as the LRA leaders

were involved in peace talks and the violence had abated. Walking through the town of Kitgum, Caroline Cox found the local people relatively relaxed and graciously friendly. She met two young men, Justin and Denis, who walked with her, talking about many different topics. Eventually she asked them about the LRA, and they both acknowledged that they had been abductees. "They certainly were not seeking sympathy or telling me a sob story," she later explained. "However, as their stories unfolded, some of the horrors they had endured were revealed."

They described how they had been forced to kill other children, including two who had tried to escape and had been recaptured. These unfortunate teenagers were strapped to the ground and other young people were forced to kill them – one was trampled to death; the other hacked to pieces. Then, the most painful admission by Justin: after he escaped he learned that the LRA had killed his father in retaliation. He will for ever carry the guilt of feeling responsible for his father's death.

Later, when Caroline and the boys arrived at the place where they would be staying, she went to find her colleague David Thomas, a chaplain in the Royal Marines, as she felt he could help them spiritually. Before the boys left, they offered to write their stories – an offer that was accepted by Caroline and David with deep appreciation.

The next day, Denis and Justin returned with immaculately written stories. On the final page there were figures, which Caroline Cox thought would be a request for some financial assistance – something she more or less expected since young people who have escaped from the LRA desperately need education to try to build a future for themselves. So as Justin haltingly read the poignant words he had written and approached the final page, she and David were expecting a request for financial help.

However, as he turned the page over, Justin said, "We wanted to give you a gift, but we have nothing to offer you. All we can give you are our favourite verses from the Bible. So here they are ... "

The figures were the chapters and verses of their most cherished biblical texts.

Caroline and David, deeply moved by the gesture, asked whether the boys had Bibles of their own. They did not – they had to borrow from friends. Caroline and David gave them their own Bibles and the two young men accepted them eagerly, immediately turning the pages to discover and share more of their favourite passages.

A Front Line in Global Jihad

It has been widely and accurately reported that Northern Uganda's LRA has long been financed by Khartoum's Islamist regime. This co-operation bolsters the belief of Baroness Cox and many other expert observers that a systemized plan continues to unfold – funded by oil-rich Saudi Arabian Wahhabists in co-operation with Khartoum's radical Muslim leadership – to Islamize the African continent by all means available: localized violence and death threats; internal immigration for demographic purposes; intimidation; proliferation of mosques; persecution of "infidels"; proselytism and forced conversions. Such efforts are generously supported by the Saudis' so-called "chequebook diplomacy".

All this unfolds beneath a black banner that has been raised around the world, unfurled and snapping in the Four Winds, heralding global jihad. War has been declared by numerous Islamic leaders, both religious and political, both Shi'a and Sunni, against all who refuse to participate in an emerging pan-Islamic nation, with Christians and Jews as their primary targets. Asymmetrical battle lines have been drawn. Initial volleys have been fired in New York, Washington DC, Bali, Madrid, London and countless other lands – most certainly including Sudan and Northern Uganda.

There is, in fact, much at stake in Northern Uganda. There is a humanitarian crisis, to be sure, as well as an urgent need for the rehabilitation of thousands of young people and their families who have suffered so severely at the hands of the LRA. But there is also a strategic front line. Northern Uganda has been identified by Khartoum as a primary target for desta-bilizing Southern Sudan, thereby softening up resistance to a global agenda to expand the pan-Islamic empire, governed by Shari'a law, southwards throughout Africa.

The following is a prescient excerpt from an SPLA report, published in October 2001 in the wake of the murders of 11 September. Even today it remains eerily current, thought-provoking and worthy of consideration.

> *Although Osama bin Laden left Sudan in 1996, he left behind a large number of his al-Qaeda members to run the training camps and businesses that are fronts for terrorist activities. The NIF government provides safe havens and diplomatic passports to members of Egyptian Gamaat al Islamia, Algerian Islamic Jihad, Hamas, and Palestinian Islamic Jihad. The GOS also trains, arms and harbours terrorists operating in the East African region, particularly in Uganda, Kenya, Tanzania, Somalia, Ethiopia and Eritrea. Some of these terrorists are involved in the jihad in Sudan. Khartoum therefore is still heavily involved in terrorism ... It has not abandoned terrorism and what the regime is now doing, in the form of co-operating with the US, is tactical and designed to hoodwink the international community ... They remain terrorists to the core.*

CHAPTER TEN

Islam and Islamism –
Reconciliation through Realism

The world awoke on 7 July 2005 to the sight of vivid red news banners spread across television screens: London Terror. And beneath those banners were gruesome scenes of the aftermath of terrorism as it unfolded – yet again – before a horrified global audience. For days afterwards the news was dominated by video loops of smouldering trains, the bombed bus split open like a tin can, mutilated casualties being rushed into ambulances, bleeding, weeping victims, and solemn, weary London police officers. Familiar tourist sites such as Big Ben, Buckingham Palace and the London Eye were juxtaposed with the desperate faces of family members in search of their lost loved ones, some of whom were dismembered beyond recognition deep beneath the city's streets.

Four suicide bombers had attacked during London's morning rush hour within minutes of each other, striking three London Underground trains and one of the city's familiar red double-decker buses. Some 56 people were confirmed dead, with more than 700 injured. It was the worst terrorist attack in the United Kingdom since the downing of Pan Am Flight 103 over Lockerbie, Scotland in 1988; the most lethal bombings there since World War II; and the first suicide bombings to strike Great Britain.

Everyone knew that London would eventually have its own 11 September. It was just a matter of time. And now it had happened. The world waited to hear what it already knew: al-Qaeda had struck again. But curiously, just hours after the explosions had once again shaken the foundations of the Western world, the British leadership was reluctant to place the responsibility where it so clearly belonged. As Douglas Davis later wrote in the *Jerusalem Post*:

> *The two words that were on everyone's lips – "Islamic" and "terrorists" – were excised from the official public discourse as effectively as Stalin airbrushed fallen comrades from group photographs. In the case of the London attacks, it would have been funny were the loss of more than 50 lives not so tragic. Within hours of the multiple, co-ordinated attacks, police spokesman Andy Paddick fired a pre-emptive broadside when confronted with a journalist's question: Were the attacks perpetrated by Islamic terrorists? "Islam", the outraged policeman shot back, "is a moderate, peace-loving religion, and the bombings, therefore, could not possibly have been the acts of true Muslims."*

> (*Jerusalem Post*, "Letter from London", 17 July 2005)

Commentator and expert on Islam Daniel Pipes wrote on 12 July:

> *Thanks to the war in Iraq, much of the world sees the British government as resolute and tough and the French one as appeasing and weak. But in another war, the one against terrorism and radical Islam, the reverse is true: France is the most stalwart nation in the West, even more so than America, while Britain is the most hapless.*

> *British-based terrorists have carried out operations in Pakistan, Afghanistan, Kenya, Tanzania, Saudi Arabia, Iraq, Israel, Morocco, Russia, Spain, and America. Many governments – Jordanian, Egyptian, Moroccan, Spanish, French, and American – have protested London's refusal to shut down its Islamist terrorist infrastructure or extradite wanted operatives. In frustration, Egypt's president Hosni Mubarak publicly denounced Britain for "protecting killers". One American security group has*

called for Britain to be listed as a terrorism-sponsoring
state.

(New York Sun, 12 July 2005).

Of course the British tendency towards political appeasement
extends far beyond today's lukewarm response to radical
Islam. It first came to the world's attention in the 1930s, when
Neville Chamberlain famously tried to negotiate with Adolf
Hitler. Yet again today, in an effort to avoid giving any offence
to any Muslims, British politicians often avoid the use of any
word that might offend, including the word "terrorism", even
after the 7 July attacks.

Despite the current fashion for rigid political correct-
ness, there are some people who have long been aware of the
growing threats posed by Islamist terrorism. As we've seen in
preceding chapters, one such member of the House of Lords,
who along with her colleagues has long sought to increase
both political and public awareness of those threats, is
Baroness Cox. She has not only watched the media reports of
increasing Islamist jihad in far-flung parts of the world, but
has witnessed its brutality at first hand and seen the devastation left behind.

After returning from her fact-finding visits, Caroline Cox
has persistently brought her eyewitness reports before
Parliament. Less than three years before terrorists struck
London, on 14 November 2002, she stood in the House of
Lords and said:

> *In 1999 I first voiced my concerns over the dangers of*
> *Islamist terrorism. Since then the horrors of September*
> *11th, the attacks on ships, the nightmare in Bali, the*
> *tragedy in Moscow, attacks on German tourists in Tunisia*
> *and French workers in Pakistan are a few examples that*
> *have hit the headlines...*
>
> *While the dreadful events on September 11th last*
> *year highlighted the danger of Islamist terrorism to*
> *Westerners, they reflected a reality that had already caused*

suffering on a huge scale in many other parts of the world. So, when President Bush and our Prime Minister described the war on terrorism as the first war of the new century, many people were surprised, including those who had already seen large numbers of their compatriots killed by Islamist terrorism..

After citing examples of such killings around the world, she continued:

Moving towards home, in Britain, there is concern that well-known Islamist militants have been recruiting and training new supporters, apparently with impunity. Although there have been some arrests, prominent leaders such as Abu Hamza al-Masri and Sheikh Omar Bakri Mohammed are still at large.

Another concern involves the financial penetration by militant Islamists of key institutions. Last year, I referred to the case of Salah Idris, the owner of a pharmaceutical factory in Sudan and therefore presumably with good relations with the Islamist NIF regime. He then owned 75 per cent of shares in the firm IES Digital Systems, which was responsible for security surveillance here in the Palace of Westminster, in British Airways and in other significant institutions. He also had a 20 per cent shareholding in Protec, a security organization with security projects in Ministry of Defence institutions and nuclear installations at Dounreay and Sellafield. I asked the Minister whether the anti-terrorism legislation prevents the financial penetration of key institutions. To date, I have received no reply...

Nearly three years later, the terrorist attack in Britain refocused the world's attention on the threats cited by those few leaders who had fearlessly spoken out, including Lady Cox in her 2002 speech. Why had there been no warnings of the attacks? How could such a target as the London transport system be so vulnerable? Above all else, who were the perpetrators?

Interestingly, on 5 July 2005, just two days before the London bombings, the Muslim cleric whom Caroline Cox had mentioned in her address to the House of Lords, Abu Hamza al-Masri, went on trial in London, facing fifteen counts, including nine of solicitation to murder. Most of those counts accused him of encouraging the murder of non-Muslims; one specifically charged him with soliciting the murder of Jews.

Less than two weeks after the London bombings, the second Muslim cleric Baroness Cox had mentioned, the fire-brand cleric Omar Bakri Mohammed, was once again preaching one of his vitriolic sermons – in London. The *San Francisco Chronicle* reported:

> *"Everything changed with the 19 magnificent terrorists of 9/11," thunders Sheikh Omar Bakri Mohammed. A raucous rejoinder of "Allah Akbar", or "God is great", rings out from the more than 60 men who fill the Collingwood Hall community center on a Saturday night in East London. The room is so crowded that some of the audience – mainly young men under 25 – must sit on the floor while others watch from the hallway.*
>
> *Long before the deadly July 7 bombings in London, Bakri's detractors warned that behind the lurid sound bites and incendiary language was an extremist whose sermons might be interpreted by his followers as justification for terrorist attacks in Britain… Though none of the suicide bombers has been linked to Bakri, his message of Islamic supremacy has reportedly inspired hundreds of young Britons to become holy warriors.*

Clearly, human rights and justice are among Caroline Cox's most prized ideals, and she is a tireless campaigner for them. When asked about her determination to see militant Islam confronted, she always begins by emphasizing the fact that "the vast majority of the world's 1.2 billion Muslims are peaceable, law-abiding and very hospitable people to whom we should extend hands of friendship". Only after this important caveat does she explain some of her concerns. Among these, she refers not only to terrorism but also to the strict Muslim legal code, Shari'a law, which traditional Muslims are obliged to implement throughout the whole world.

"Shari'a law", she explains, "is not compatible with the Universal Declaration of Human Rights: it does not allow freedom to choose and change religion. You can become a Muslim, but if you stop being a Muslim and you convert to another religion, you run the risk of the death sentence for apostasy. Shari'a simply does not permit equality before the law, not only between Muslims and non-Muslims but also between men and women."

Even as she speaks about the encroachment of Shari'a law around the world, the circumstances of Christians in Muslim lands have continued to be a cause for concern. The *Jerusalem Post Christian Edition* reported some examples of the ongoing problems encountered by Christians in Muslim lands in February 2007:

> *In Iraq: In October 2006, Father Boulos Iskander, 59, a Syrian Orthodox priest, was beheaded in a town near Mosul. His kidnappers had demanded $40,000 and that the priest's church publicly repudiate Pope Benedict XVI's recent remarks about Islam. In November a bomb blast shattered the windows of a Catholic church in Mosul while Dominican priests were holding evening prayer. Tens of thousands of Christians have fled Iraq since the war began in 2003.*
>
> *In Malaysia: In November 2006 angry Muslims protested outside Our Lady of Lourdes Catholic Church in Ipoh, Perak State, after word spread that the church would baptize a group of Malay Muslims who had converted to Christianity. Earlier in the year, a Malaysian female convert to Christianity was forced into hiding after Muslim radicals issued death threats against her and the lawyers representing her case. Islamic laws in Malaysia forbid conversion out of Islam ("apostasy") and regard it as a*

criminal offense; "apostates" may be fined, detained and imprisoned.

In Turkey: In November 2006, six Molotov cocktails damaged a Protestant place of worship in western Turkey breaking windows and scorching the exterior of the building. The attack followed months of repeated harassment of Christians in the town of Odemis, 65 miles east of Izmir. In a more recent incident, Asia News reported, "Turan Topal and Hakan Tastan, two converts to Christianity, are facing trial on November 23, and could get six months to three years in prison." Their crime? "Insulting Turkishness."

In Egypt: "An Egyptian Christian teenager escaped her Muslim kidnappers in October 2006 hours after they had drugged her on a public bus. They threatened to rape her and convert her to Islam if her family did not leave their Nile Delta city of El-Mahala el-Kobra. Laurence Wagih Emil, fifteen, escaped the ground-floor room where she was being held in Cairo's southern Helwan suburb at 10 p.m. while her captors were away breaking their Ramadan fast" (Compass Direct). Egypt's Coptic and Evangelical Christians face enormous social pressure, intimidation and threats of violence.

In Iran: The World Evangelical Alliance Religious Liberty Prayer List reports, "On 10 December 2006 Iranian secret police raided Christian fellowships in Karaj, Tehran, Rasht and Bandar-i Anzali, confiscating computers, literature and materials and arresting fifteen believers they accused of evangelism and actions against the national security of Iran. All but one have since been released after forfeiting money, job permits and even house deeds as bail. Reportedly, new government directives will soon place the church even more under the thumb of the intelligence ministry and security forces." [http://www.ea.org.au/rlc/]

In Ethiopia: Increasing anti-Christian violence was spearheaded by radical Muslims from Somalia, who declared jihad *against Ethiopian Christians.* World Magazine *reported on October 10 2006, "For weeks a group of about 300 men the locals described as 'Muslim fundamentalists' trained in a remote area near the town of Jima, 250 miles southwest of Addis Ababa. According to eyewitnesses, the group includes a number of Somalis. Government forces, alarmed by their activities, arrested several of the leaders. But the remainder organized and, armed with machetes and knives, attacked Christian churches and villages. Two months later, in a stunning turnaround, the Ethiopian army not only drove the jihadists out of Ethiopia, but as* The Guardian *reported on December 27, 2006, "pushed to within 18 miles of the Islamist stronghold of Mogadishu today..." Despite the fact that the Ethiopians were responding to an invasion of their sovereign state, however, "international criticism of their incursion into Somalia mounted".*

Reconciliation through Realism – February, 2007

Against this backdrop, in February 2007, Baroness Cox addressed a conference organized by the National Research Council in Rome. In the text that accompanied her speech, prepared with her colleague the researcher John Marks, Caroline Cox formally expressed her views with regard to Islam and Islamism. In the pages that follow, her words serve as a fitting conclusion to this chapter and, in a broader sense, to this book.

There are over a billion Muslims in the world today. The vast majority lead law-abiding lives and live peaceably with their neighbours, including those of other faiths. In many countries, Muslims are respected for their hospitality and graciousness and have lived harmoniously with those around them for centuries.

Some nation states, such as Indonesia – which is the world's largest Islamic nation – and Nigeria, have enshrined the principles of cultural pluralism and religious tolerance in their constitutions. The words "Unity in Diversity" are inscribed in Indonesia's national emblem. A similar principle underpins the federal constitution in Nigeria since independence in 1960; the same is true of the secular state of Turkey.

Other Islamic nations such as Jordan, Oman and the UAE respect fundamental freedoms, such as freedom of worship. In these countries, relationships between Muslims and those of other faiths, such as Christians and traditional believers, have long been harmonious. Mutual respect, friendship and shared participation in community events, such as weddings, are evident.

But recent years have seen the development of more violent movements in some countries, with bitter conflict, fighting, death and destruction. As we've seen in previous pages, in Sudan the toll of human suffering is the greatest in the world today. With over 2 million dead and over 5 million displaced, the scale of human misery in Sudan exceeds that of Somalia, Rwanda and former Yugoslavia taken together. Likewise northern Nigeria – despite the wording of Nigeria's constitution – has been afflicted with violent intercommunal conflict associated with the imposition of Shari'a law – now implemented in twelve of its 36 states. And – it bears repeating – parts of Indonesia, such as Maluku, Sulawesi and Aceh, have also suffered, with thousands of innocent civilians killed and hundreds of thousands displaced.

In recent years many countries have also seen terrorist attacks in the name of Islam or Islamism. One of many problems caused by such terrorism is a rise in indiscriminate fear and dislike of all Muslims. Therefore, it is essential to make distinctions between law-abiding and peaceable Muslims and militant Islamists. Moreover, unless we are seen to be taking Islamist terrorism seriously, there will be a backlash against all Muslims, for terrorism breeds fear and fear can blur distinctions. Hence there is an urgent need for well-informed understanding of the nature of Islam, as well as a clear definition of militant Islamism. Taking these important matters seriously will help to prevent tensions between communities in countries such as Britain and other European nations, forestall the outbreak or resurgence of conflict in regions where this is incipient, and may also help to encourage reconciliation once conflict has broken out.

Some Causes of Conflict

Many Muslims are deeply concerned about certain negative characteristics of Western societies. These criticisms include the following beliefs and allegations: Western societies are morally decadent. They are inherently and fundamentally prejudiced against Islam and Muslims. Historically, they launched the medieval Crusades in a bid to eliminate Islam, and they are now launching a modern crusade with the same aim. They support the state of Israel. And they are allies of America, which has based its troops in the Islamic holy land of Saudi Arabia since 1990.

Some of these criticisms and concerns may well be valid: the statistics of family breakdown, crime and juvenile delinquency in the West reflect many deep social problems. But in pressing these criticisms, many Muslims show a great reluctance to appreciate the positive aspects of Western societies, such as the freedom to speak and criticize, or the freedom to practice religion. Meanwhile, these same Muslims may often be unwilling to allow any criticism of Islamic societies.

Traditional Islamic regimes, such as Saudi Arabia, Iran, the Taliban or the National Islamic Front (NIF) in Sudan, are fiercely intolerant of dissent, and, *de facto*, lacking in individual freedoms. Control is attempted over all aspects of life – political, economic, cultural, educational, religious and military – and is frequently enforced centrally in the name of Islam or Islamism. Freedom of expression, and of access to information, are rigidly controlled, since conformity with the dominant ideology is the central value. Such hegemony is rooted in the nature of orthodox Islam, which does not differentiate between the personal and the political, and which prescribes behaviour conforming to Islamic principles in every aspect of life. Consequently, within such regimes, no effective checks or balances exist on the exercise of power by the ruling or governing religious group. Such comprehensive domination by religion of virtually every aspect of human life, individual and collective, enshrines totalitarian control – control that is incompatible with the ideals of individual freedom that lie at the heart of liberal democracy.

The Shari'a legal system was developed in early Islamic societies. In one form or another, its application is often urged on societies in the modern world if they are to be truly Islamic. As Bernard Lewis has written, "The Shari'a is simply the law, and there is no other. It is holy in that it derives from God, and is the external and unchangeable expression of God's commandments to mankind."

In a *Commentary* article titled "Islam versus Democracy" (January 1993) Martin Kramer wrote that Shari'a law contains:

> *... principled affirmations of inequality, primarily between Muslims and non-Muslims, secondarily between men and women. This has made fundamentalists into the most unyielding critics of the Universal Declaration of Human Rights, which guarantees the freedom to choose one's religion and one's spouse. Both freedoms indisputably contradict Islamic law, which defines conversion out of Islam as a capital offence, and forbids marriage between a Muslim woman and a non-Muslim man ...*
>
> *The Shari'a, as a perfect law, cannot be abrogated or altered, and certainly not by the shifting moods of an electorate. Accordingly, every major fundamentalist thinker has repudiated popular sovereignty as a rebellion against God, the sole legislator. In the changed circumstances of the 1990s, some activists do allow that an election can*

> *serve a useful one-time purpose, as a collective referen-*
> *dum of allegiance to Islam, and as an act of submission*
> *to a regime of divine justice. But once such a regime gains*
> *power, its true measure is not how effectively it imple-*
> *ments the will of the people but how efficiently it applies*
> *Islamic law.*

Just as the word "Shari'a" has recently become familiar to Western ears, so has the word *jihad*.

"Jihad" has various meanings. Literally it means "strug-gle", including "struggle for the good Islamic life". But "jihad" is also translated as "holy war", and it often means *violent* holy war. Islamist literature frequently mentions jihad for various purposes, and that very ambiguity leaves it open to different interpretations.

According to Bernard Lewis, in his book *The Political Language of Islam*, jihad is:

> *... an Arabic word with the literal meaning of "effort,"*
> *"striving," or "struggle". In the Qur'an and still more the*
> *Traditions commonly though not invariably followed by*
> *the words "in the path of God", it has usually been under-*
> *stood as meaning "to wage war". The great collections of*
> *hadith all contain a section devoted to jihad in which the*
> *military meaning predominates. The same is true of the*
> *classical manuals of Shari'a law. There were some who*
> *argued that jihad should be understood in a moral and*
> *spiritual, rather than a military, sense. Such arguments*
> *were sometimes put forward by Shi'ite theologians in clas-*
> *sical times, and more frequently by modernizers and*
> *reformists in the nineteenth and twentieth centuries. The*
> *overwhelming majority of classical theologians, jurists,*
> *and traditionalists, however, understood the obligation of*
> *jihad in a military sense, and have examined and*
> *expounded it accordingly.*
>
> *... jihad, is one of the basic commandments of the*
> *faith, an obligation imposed on all Muslims by God,*

through revelation… The basis of the obligation of jihad is the universality of the Muslim revelation. God's word and God's message are for all mankind; it is the duty of those who have accepted them to strive (jahada) unceasingly to convert or at least to subjugate those who have not. This obligation is without limit of time or space. It must continue until the whole world has either accepted the Islamic faith or submitted to the power of the Islamic state.

Until that happens, the world is divided into two: the House of Islam (dar al-Islam), where Muslims rule and the law of Islam prevails; and the House of War (dar al-Harb), comprising the rest of the world. Between the two there is a morally necessary, legally and religiously obligatory state of war, until the final and inevitable triumph of Islam over unbelief. According to the law books, this state of war could be interrupted, when expedient, by an armistice or truce of limited duration. It could not be terminated by a peace, but only by a final victory.

Jihad **and the Koran**

A key development in the concept of jihad is contained in this verse in the Koran:

Fight those who believe not in Allah, nor the Last Day, nor hold that forbidden which has been forbidden by Allah and His Prophet, nor acknowledge the religion of truth (i.e. Islam) among the People of the Book (Jews and Christians), until they pay the jizya *(tax) with willing submission, and feel themselves subdued. (Sura 9:29, Medina)*

In other words these Koranic teachings require Muslims to fight unbelievers – those who allow things Allah forbids – and specifically Jews and Christians, unless they pay the *jizya* tax. The options for other unbelievers are to accept Islam or be killed. Jihad is also waged against apostates or Muslims who seek to change their religion. Their options are recantation or death. In Mohammed's time, jihad was practised regularly against Christians and Jews as well as against those who did not convert to Islam. As the Koran says: "... if they turn renegades, seize them and slay them wherever ye find them (Sura 4:89, Medina).

It must be noted that there are other verses in the Koran that speak of peace and respect for other people, especially "People of the Book" – Jews and Christians. For example, this Sura: "And argue not with the people of the Scripture (Jews and Christians), unless it be (in a way) that is better (with good words and in a good manner, inviting them to Islamic monotheism with His Verses). Except with such of them as do wrong, and say (to them): "We believe in that which has been revealed to you, our Ilah (God) and your Ilah (God) is One ... " (29:46, Mecca).

However, traditional Islamic teaching has resolved any inconsistency between the verses of peace and the verses of war by adopting the principle of "abrogation", whereby the later revelations to the Prophet abrogate, or override, the earlier revelations. Unfortunately this means that the more aggressive militaristic interpretation of *jihad*, associated with violence and terrorism, prevails over peaceable interpretations. Such militaristic interpretations are often voiced as a justification for terrorist activities by those who undertake them. It is disturbing that an increasing number of such dedicated terrorists are now born in Western countries and have been indoctrinated with this violent interpretation of Islam in their own homelands.

Jihad and the Promise of Paradise

Muslims believe that when they die they go to the grave to await the Day of Judgment, when Allah will decide, on the basis of works done on earth, who goes to Paradise and who to hell. The only way to guarantee going to Paradise is to die in jihad while fighting the enemies of Islam. This provides a major religious motive for suicide bombers or to otherwise volunteer for jihad.

The ultimate aim of jihad is to establish Islamic authority over the whole world, as indicated by this Koranic verse: "And fight with them on until there is no more tumult and oppression, And there prevail justice and faith in Allah all together and everywhere … " (Sura 8:39, Medina).

Over 22 years (610–632), Mohammed's precepts in the Koran changed from a requirement to fight those who persecute you, to fight those who reject Islam in Arabia, to the final command of jihad – conquer the world in the name of Islam. No subsequent Koranic verse contradicts this final command of jihad, and so it remains a goal of many Muslims today.

Over the centuries that followed Mohammad's life jihad was remarkably successful. Starting with the capture of Jerusalem from the Christians in 638, followed by the capture of much of Spain by 715 – a conquest that did not finally end until the fall of Granada in 1492, nearly 800 years later – Islam first conquered and then converted much of Europe, North Africa and Asia. Overall this jihad lasted nearly 1,300 years, until the nineteenth century, interrupted only by about 200 years of resistance during the Crusades (1096–1270).

Many non-Muslims, and especially Christians, often express guilt about the history of the Crusades. In so doing, they are taking them out of context: they fail to understand that the Crusades were a response to 450 years of Islamic aggression and conquest, during which Christendom and Judaism lost the historic lands of the Bible, much of North Africa and an increasing part of Europe: Islam had advanced to the north of Spain and into central France, where its armies were defeated near Poitiers.

The modern accusation, therefore, that Christians were the primary aggressors is invalid. It is true that atrocities were perpetrated by both Christians and Muslims, and the ruthlessness of some of the destruction of life and property during the Crusades – Christian, Muslim and Jewish – is entirely unacceptable, especially by modern standards. But such practices were carried out by both sides and were not unusual for that era. Therefore, when Muslims accuse Christians of being guilty of the Crusades, it is important to respond with an accurate and appropriate reminder of the history of the Islamic aggression that preceded the Crusades.

Human Rights and Religious Freedoms in Traditional Islam

In her book *Islam and Human Rights: Tradition and Politics*, author A. Mayer has compared the 1948 United Nations Universal Declaration of Human Rights with a number of documents setting out Islam's attitude to alternative ideologies and dissent, including:

- A pamphlet by Mawdudi (a Pakistani Islamist who died in 1979);
- The 1981 Universal Islamic Declaration of Human Rights;
- A draft Islamic Constitution published by Al-Azhar University in Cairo;
- The 1979 Iranian Constitution.

In summary, Mayer concludes that:

> ... the Shari'a criteria that are employed to restrict rights are left so uncertain and general that they ... afford no means for protecting the individual against deprivations of the rights that are guaranteed by international law. Thereby the stage is set not just for the diminution of these rights but potentially for denying them altogether.

Freedom of Religion and Apostasy

As we've seen, the traditional Islamic response to Muslims who seek to change their religion is recantation or death. Moreover, there is no indication that any of the modern Islamic authorities analysed by Mayer regard this as a problem:

> ... The failure of a single one of these Islamic human rights schemes to take a position against the application of the Shari'a death penalty for apostasy means that the authors of these schemes have neglected to confront and resolve the main issues involved in harmonizing international human rights and Shari'a standards.

The Status of Women

The status of women within Islam is a major matter of diverse interpretations. What is clear is that there are considerable limitations on what women can do compared with men, both in the home and in public. Most crucially, in courts of law on many key issues the testimony of one man is equivalent to that of two women. Also, in a Shari'a court, a woman accused of adultery is required to have four male witnesses in her defence. If found guilty, she is liable to be sentenced to death by stoning.

There is no indication that most Islamic authorities regard the rights of women as a problem. According to Mayer:

> ... there is an absence of any willingness to recognize women as full, equal human beings who deserve the same rights and freedoms as men. Instead, discrimination against women is treated as something entirely natural ...

The Rights of Non-Muslims and Dhimmi Status

Throughout the history of Islamic societies non-Muslims have been given a less advantageous status than that granted to

Muslims. This *dhimmi* system has been applied most frequently to Jews and Christians. They were able to live within Islamic societies, sometimes in peace, provided they accepted *dhimmi* status, which involved paying a special tax and having considerably fewer legal rights than Muslims. For example they were limited in the ability to own property or to carry out certain occupations. Even today in Islamic courts of law they are not allowed to give evidence against Muslims and often have to pay a Muslim to give evidence for them.

Mayer concluded, from the Islamic documents she analysed:

> ... to the extent that they deal with the question of the rights of religious minorities, they seem to endorse pre-modern Shari'a rules that call for non-Muslims to be relegated to an inferior status if they qualify as members of the ahl al-kitab *(i.e. Jews or Christians), and for them to be treated as non-persons if they do not qualify for such inclusion. The Azhar draft constitution avoids dealing with the status of non-Muslims. In the context of a document that seems to support the general applicability of pre-modern Shari'a rules, the failure to address the issue suggests that the intent was to retain such rules to govern the status of non-Muslims.*

Moderate Muslim Voices

In the face of Islamist extremism and terrorism, the need for reform in Islam is much discussed and sought after, and not only by non-Muslims. Reform is recognized as an urgent necessity by some prominent modern Muslims thinkers. One is Tariq Ali, writing in *The Clash of Fundamentalisms: Crusades, Jihads and Modernity*:

> We are in desperate need of an Islamic Reformation that sweeps away the crazed conservatism and backwardness of the fundamentalists but, more than that, opens up the

world of Islam to new ideas which are seen to be more advanced than what is currently on offer from the West. This would necessitate a rigid separation of state and mosque; the dissolution of the clergy; the assertion by Muslim intellectuals of their right to interpret the texts that are the collective property of Islamic culture as a whole; the freedom to think freely and rationally and the freedom of imagination. Unless we move in this direction we will be doomed to re-living old battles, and thinking not of a richer and humane future, but of how we can move from the present to the past. It is an unacceptable vision.

Another Muslim who is trying to interpret Islam in ways that allow peaceful co-existence and self-critical enquiry is Irshad Manji, whose early experiences in a *madrassah* in Vancouver, Canada led her to become what she calls a Muslim "refusenik". In her book *The Trouble With Islam: A Muslim's Call for Reform in Her Faith*, she writes: "That doesn't mean I refuse to be a Muslim, it simply means I refuse to join an army of automatons in the name of Allah." Manji argues that "a liberal Islamic reformation" is long overdue and suggests that Muslims living in the West are best placed to bring this about. The final chapter of her book is titled, "Thank God for the West".

There are also some Muslims in Islamic countries who are both opposed to militant Islamism and who are courageously prepared to say so publicly. These include, for example, former presidents Megawati Sukarnoputri and Abdurrahman Wahid in Indonesia. Meanwhile, many Muslims in Sudan have consistently opposed the Islamist regime in Khartoum since it seized power in 1989 and declared jihad against all who oppose it.

Two recent African examples of such public opposition focus on both militant Islamism and the role of Saudi Arabia in exporting *Wahhabism* to other countries.

The first, from Ethiopia, is *Saudi Arabia's Wahhabism and the Threat to Ethiopia's National Security*, published on 26

September 2003 by Ethiopian journalist Alem-Zelalem. He describes how Saudi Arabia's *Wahhabist* interpretation of Islam has corrupted the Islam of his native Ethiopia:

> ... the great majority of Ethiopian Muslims are followers of Sunni Islam. Since there is religious tolerance in the country, Ethiopians have managed to escape destructive religious conflicts, which have become prevalent in many parts of the world. Lately, however, there has been a new development in the country, which, unless timely measures are taken to check it, could ultimately be a destabilizing factor in the region. This destabilizing factor, which, next to oil, has become the major export item of Saudi Arabia, is called Wahhabism. As the whole world knows, Saudi Arabia is a fundamentalist state. The type of Islam that it preaches and practices is not [the] Sunni Islam that we have lived with for centuries in Ethiopia, and that has become an integral part of our culture and history, but Wahhabism – a terrorist and violent form of Islam – that is responsible for the slaughter of thousands of innocent lives throughout the world.

The second example, from Somalia, is an article entitled "Against the Saudization of Somaliland", published on 21 November 2003 by Somalian journalist Bashir Goth. Goth writes:

> Recently, I came across news reports on the activities of a group of clerics calling themselves "the Authority for Promotion of Virtue and Prevention of Vice" trying to impose draconian moral codes on Somaliland citizens. I cannot sit back and watch these people humiliate our women, destroy our beautiful culture, hijack our religion, and denigrate the reputation of our country worldwide.

Goth recalls a time:

> ... when Islam and the Somali culture lived together in perfect harmony; when being Somali and Muslim was an

*indivisible whole. It was a time when the message of tol-
erance and peace prevailed. One could pray occasionally,
or never pray at all, fast in the month of Ramadan or never
fast at all, make a pilgrimage to Mecca or never do it at all;
but would forever consider oneself a true follower of
Islam …*

Such concerns could be repeated in many African countries.

Finally, within Saudi Arabia itself, the writings of Saudi
journalist Raid Qusti, a columnist for the Saudi English daily
Arab News, are of interest. Qusti has written columns in favour
of expanding women's rights, educational reform and modern-
ization, and is often critical of Islamism. In his articles Qusti
has criticized "many Muslim scholars" for having "a mindset
of the distant past".

On 21 May, 2003 Qusti wrote an article in *Arab News*
entitled "We Need to Learn to Be Self-Critical". In it he wrote:

*… ask any decent journalist in the world what he does for
a living and the answer will come: "Seeking the truth."
However, seeking the truth and reporting the facts, as we
journalists know, comes at a cost … being a journalist or
writer in Saudi Arabia, especially for a major Saudi
English newspaper read worldwide, comes at double, if
not triple the cost … it was only when I started writing
about Saudi society and speaking about it candidly that I
realized that self-criticism in Saudi Arabia is sometimes
considered unpatriotic. Why? Because as a Saudi writing
in English, my writings, which criticize what I believe is
wrong in our society, are considered by many here – especially the conservatives – as giving free ammunition to our
enemies …*

*… I am a journalist like my father and my grandfa-
ther before me. Journalism runs in my blood. I am also a
Saudi citizen who is patriotic and loves his country. You
or others might criticize what I and others say in the local
press, but I remain defiant. No country in the world can*

progress or develop without being self-critical. It is unfortunate that we Saudis have to learn that the hard way.

The Challenge to Western Societies

Militant Islamism is growing in Western societies. Only a small minority of Muslims in countries such as Britain adhere overtly to Islamist beliefs and practices. Yet their commitment to the use of any means, including terrorism, to destroy Western societies is a threat that must be addressed.

For example, in August 1999 a film was shown on *Dispatches* on England's Channel 4, in which Abu Hamza and Sheikh Bakri Mohammed adjure a large audience of young men not to believe in the laws of Great Britain, but only to observe the laws of Allah. These clerics are shown virulently promoting violence: for example, in one case they demonstrate ways of using nets with explosives to bring down civilian aircraft making their descent into a London airport. More insidiously, these radical voices claim that this "Islamic Anti-Aircraft Net" is just one example of a terrorist device and they then encourage each young man present to go and develop his own terrorist tactic for the jihad. It is, they say, a question of "kill or be killed".

Unfortunately, this was not a one-off event. Previously, young men trained in Britain had been sent to Yemen to carry out a terrorist attack. Subsequently, a young British man – Richard Reid – tried to blow up an American civilian airliner with a shoe-bomb. Analysis of some of the more militant Islamic websites in Britain and elsewhere indicates the intensity of militant beliefs and the subversive policies that are being widely disseminated.

The Response of Liberal Democracies

There is clearly a need for democratic societies to respond to those who use the freedoms of democracy to destroy democracy itself and the freedoms it enshrines. The challenge is to confront such threats in ways that are not incompatible with the freedoms and values of the liberal democracy we are trying to defend.

The ideals and institutions of Western societies must be articulated clearly. The peoples of the world can then emulate or reject those values and institutions on the basis of knowledge rather than ignorance. Only thus will all people be free to choose their own religious commitments and political systems.

The time has also come for those who live in democratic societies to use wisdom and discernment in responding to political and economic initiatives proposed by Muslim leaders – initiatives that are designed to curtail or destroy the fundamental freedoms on which democracies are based. One British example illustrates the need for vigilance and principled response: attempts to inhibit fundamental freedoms of speech under the guise of legislation purporting to prevent "Incitement to Religious Hatred".

No one in the British Parliament wishes to condone incitement to religious hatred and thus it seemed invidious to challenge this proposed legislation, promoted by the Muslim Council of Britain and supported by the Labour government. However, close scrutiny and shrewd analysis revealed a hidden agenda: the new law, if passed, would criminalize (with potential prison sentences of up to seven years) any criticism of or jokes about Islam, and any proselytizing of any other religion.

When the bills came to the House of Lords, a broad coalition of opposition had been formed, including the National Secular Society, well-known writers and humorists, such as Rowan Atkinson ("Mr Bean" of TV fame), and many Christian groups, especially the African, Afro-Caribbean and Asian churches. These mobilized large demonstrations outside Parliament, with placards urging the need to protect freedom of speech and freedom to choose and change religion; they also sang hymns so loudly that the music of "Amazing Grace" and other songs wafted into the Palace of Westminster. Amendments to protect these fundamental freedoms were passed in the House of Lords; the Labour government was determined to remove them when the bills returned to the House of Commons. On the crucial day of voting in the House of Commons, the black church leaders again mobilized their communities for another musical demonstration as well as lobbying Labour Members of Parliament, persuading nine that afternoon to oppose the removal of the amendments. When the two key votes were taken, the first was lost by ten votes and the second by just a single vote.

On such a thin thread hung the protection of fundamental freedoms in British democracy in 2006. This example illustrates the need for vigilance, and the need to recognize when the time has come to draw a line in the sand: to say that, while we in Britain value cultural diversity and enshrine the principle of tolerance, we must also ensure that such values and principles are not used in ways that destroy the fundamental freedoms on which our democracy is built.

A Challenge to the Christian Church

One of the reasons that Islam is growing very fast in Western countries lies in the search by many people for a meaningful, coherent and inspirational faith. Western churches are often seen as divided, introverted, anachronistic – and irrelevant to the modern day. The phrase "If the trumpet gives an uncertain sound" seems to apply to the church in the West, which is split in so many ways, between and within different denominations.

Alongside the shortage of inspirational Christian leadership in the Western churches, there is the enormous influence of pop culture, with "show-biz" stars or soccer players as the most widely promoted heroes and heroines for huge fan clubs. If these are the role models that dominate youth culture, it is perhaps not surprising if many young people, who seek a more idealistic vision for inspiration on which to base their lives, find Islam a more convincing alternative. That may be one reason why it is the fastest-growing religion in Britain.

There is therefore an urgent need to develop prayerful, spiritual strategic responses to militant and political Islam. These range from prayers for wisdom and discernment to practical tactics, such as appropriate reactions to proposals that seek to implement Shari'a law.

The Bible reminds us that, without a vision, things fall apart and the people perish. We must therefore also develop an inspirational Christian vision for our countries and for the world, so that all people can have a genuine choice of religious commitment. We have seen how religious intolerance is growing and religious freedoms are increasingly under threat in many parts of the world. We also know that only the truth can make us free. Let us therefore not fear to proclaim the truth as we have received it from our forefathers, often at great cost. And with God's help, let us pass it on undiminished as a precious heritage to our children and our children's children.

Bibliography

Chapter One: Appointment with the World

K Jacka, C Cox & J Marks, *The Rape of Reason: The Corruption of the Polytechnic of North London*, Churchill Press, 1975.

C Cox & J Marks (Eds), *The Right to Learn, Centre for Policy Studies*, 1981.

C Cox, *Sociology: A Guide for Nurses, Midwives and Health Visitors*, Butterworth, 1983

Chapter Two: Poland, Romania, Russia—The Iron Hand of Communism

J Douglas-Home, *Once Upon Another Time: Ventures Behind the Iron Curtain*, Michael Russell, 2000.

B Day, *The Velvet Philosophers*, Claridge Press, 1999.

J Marks, *Fried Snowballs: Communism in Theory and Practice*, Claridge Press, 1990.

C Cox, *Cox's Book of Modern Saints and Martyrs*, Continuum, 2006.

Chapter Three: Nagorno-Karabakh—Flashpoint in an Explosive Region

C Walker, *Visions of Ararat: Writings on Armenia*, I B Tauris, 2005

G Chalian, C Walker, C Mutafian, and P Donabedian,
     Armenia and the Karabagh: The Struggle for Unity,
     Minority Rights Group, 1991.

Chapter Four: Burma—"Land without Evil"

B Rogers, *A Land Without Evil: Stopping the Genocide of
     Burma's Karen People*, Monarch Books, 2004.
C Cox & J Marks, *This Immoral Trade: Slavery in the 21st
     Century*, Monarch Books; November, 2006.
Catwalk to the Barracks: Conscription of women for sexual
     slavery and other practices of sexual violence by troops
     of the Burmese military regime in Mon areas, Woman
     and Child Rights Project (Southern Burma) in
     collaboration with Human Rights Foundation of
     Monland (Burma), July 2005.
License to Rape: The Burmese military regime's use of sexual
     violence in the ongoing war in Shan State, The Shan
     Human Rights Foundation (SHRF) and The Shan
     Women's Action Network (SWAN), May 2002.
Shattering Silences: Karen Women speak out about the
     Burmese Military Regime's use of Rape as a Strategy of
     War in Karen State, The Karen Women's Organization
     (KWO) with the collaboration of The Committee for
     Internally Displaced Karen People (CIDKP), The
     Karen Information Center (KIC), The Karen Human
     Rights Group (KHRG) and The Mergui-Tavoy District
     Information Department, April, 2004.
Driven Away: Trafficking of Kachin women on the China-
     Burma border, Kachin Women's Association of
     Thailand (KWAT), June 2005.
Physicians for Human Rights, *No Status, Migration,
     Trafficking and Exploitation of Women in Thailand*:
     Health and HIV/AIDS Risks for Burmese and Hill Tribe
     Women and Girls, Cambridge, MA, June 2004.

My Gun Was As Tall As Me: Child Soldiers in Burma, Human
Rights Watch, Chicago, October, 2002.

J Mawdsley, *The Heart Must Break: The Fight for Democracy
and Truth in Burma*, Century, 2001.

Chapter Five: Indonesia—Martyrs and Miracles

G Barton, *Gus Dur: The Authorized Biography of
Abdurrahman Wahid*, Equinox Publishing, 2005

P Riddell, *Islam in the Malay-Indonesian World* (Hardcover),
C Hurst & Co. 2001.

A Azra , *Indonesia, Islam, and Democracy: Dynamics in a
Global Context*, Solstice Publishing, 2006.

K Hidayat and A Gaus (Eds), *Islam, the State & Civil Society:
Contemporary Islamic Movements and Thought*,
LibForAll Foundation, 2005.

Chapter Six: East Timor—A Hungry Little Land

C Pinto and M Jardine, *East Timor's Unfinished Struggle:
Inside the Timorese Resistance*, South End Press, 1996.

K Gusmao, *A Woman of Independence: A story of love and the
birth of a new nation*, Macmillan, 2003.

A Kohen, *From the Place of the Dead: The Epic Struggles of
Bishop Belo of East Timor*, St Martin's Press, 1999.

J Martinkus, *A Dirty Little War*, Random House, 2001.

I Cristalis, *Bitter Dawn: East Timor - a people's story,* Zed
Books, 2002.

Chapter Seven: Nigeria—"Will You Tell the World?

J Azumah, *The Legacy of Arab-Islam in Africa: A Quest for
Inter-religious Dialogue*, Oneworld Publications, 2001.

M Hiskett, *Some to Mecca Turn to Pray: Islamic Values and the Modern World*, Claridge Press, 1993.

P Lovejoy & J Hogendorn, *Slow death for slavery: The course of abolition in Northern Nigeria, 1897-1936*, Cambridge University Press, 1993.

Chapter Eight: Sudan—Frontline against Islamists

M Nazer with D Lewis, *Slave: The True Story of a Girl's Lost Childhood and Her Fight for Survival*, Virago, 2004.

C Cox & J Marks, *This Immoral Trade: Slavery in the 21st Century*, Monarch Books, 2006.

B Lewis, *Race and Slavery in the Middle East: An Historical Enquiry*, Oxford University Press, 1990.

J Azumah, *The Legacy of Arab-Islam in Africa: A Quest for Inter-religious Dialogue*, Oneworld Publications, 2001.

J Azumah, *Islam and Slavery*, Centre for Islamic Studies, London School of Theology, 1999.

P Lovejoy, *Transformations in slavery: A history of slavery in Africa (Second Edition)*, Cambridge University Press, 2000.

M Gordon, *Slavery in the Arab World*, New Amsterdam Books, 1987.

P Manning, *Slavery and African life: Occidental, Oriental and African Slave Trades*, Cambridge University Press, 1990.

R Segal, *Islam's Black Slaves: The other black diaspora*, Farrar, Straus and Giroux, 2001

Chapter Nine: Northern Uganda—"Terrorists to the Core"

O Otunnu, *Ending Wars Against Children*, Sydney Peace Prize lecture, November 2005.

C Cox & J Marks, *This Immoral Trade: Slavery in the 21st Century*, Monarch Books, 2006.

Chapter Ten: Islam and Islamism—Reconciliation through Realism

C Cox & J Marks, *The 'West', Islam and Islamism: Is ideological Islam compatible with liberal democracy* (2nd Edition), Civitas, 2006.

A Bostom, *The Legacy of Jihad: Islamic Holy War and the Fate of Non-Muslims*, Prometheus, 2005.

A Hirsi Ali, *The Caged Virgin: An Emancipation Proclamation for Women and Islam*, Free Press, 2006.

B Tibi, *The Challenge of Fundamentalism: Political Islam and the New World Disorder*, University of California Press, 2002.

Bat Ye'or, *Eurabia*, Associated University Presses, 2005.

Belteshazzar & Abednego, *The Mosque and its Role in Society*, Pilcrow, 2006.

B Bawer, *While Europe Slept: How Radical Islam is Destroying the West from Within*, Doubleday, 2006.

C Cox with C Butcher, *Cox's Book of Modern Saints & Martyrs*, Continuum, 2006.

C Cox & J Marks, *Islam, Islamism and the West*, American Foreign Policy Council, 2005.

C Cox & J Marks, *This Immoral Trade: Slavery in the 21st Century*, Monarch Books, 2006.

E Kohlmann, *Al-Qaida's Jihad in Europe: The Afghan-Bosnian Network*, Berg, 2004.

G Barton, *Gus Dur: The Authorised Biography of Abdurrahman Wahid*, Equinox, 2002.

H Storhaug, *Human Visas*, Kolofon AS, Oslo, 2005.

Ibn Warraq, *Leaving Islam: Apostates Speak Out*, Prometheus Books, 2003.

L Vidino, *Al Qaeda in Europe: The New Battleground of International Jihad*, Prometheus, 2006.

Index

If you enjoyed this you may also appreciate:

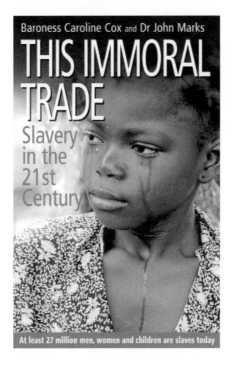

Baroness Caroline Cox and Dr John Marks

THIS IMMORAL TRADE
Slavery in the 21st Century

At least 27 million men, women and children are slaves today

Slavery remains rampant worldwide, despite the celebrations surrounding the bicentenary of its 'abolition'. At least 27m men, women and children are enslaved today, ranging from prostitutes in London to indentured workers in Burma.

This popularly written but carefully researched volume includes chapters on the causes of slavery, on the history of the practice, on different forms of contemporary slavery, and on the Christian roots of the anti-slavery movement; and three shocking case studies from Sudan, Burma and Uganda.

This Immoral Trade
Baroness Caroline Cox and Dr John Marks

ISBN: 978-1-85424-765-0 (UK)
ISBN: 978-0-8254-6131-6 (USA)

Available from your local Christian bookshop.
In case of difficulty, please visit our website: www.lionhudson.com